Praise for
Jesus in Shorts

Few people love Jesus *and* other people as much as Laura Padgett. Few writers can see Him in others, and then put those life experiences into just the right words—and in just the right portions as Laura does here. So take a seat as this gifted servant leads a step-by-step journey to meet the Prince of Peace and a host of those who know and love Him. Many life lessons reside in these glorious pages. Thank you, Laura Padgett, for crafting such a beautiful ride.

—Patricia Raybon, author of *My First White Friend and I Told the Mountain to Move*

Through her book, *Jesus in Shorts*, Laura Padgett reveals her inner truth with courageous honesty. Each chapter speaks to her life experience and her relationship with Jesus on a day-to-day basis—whether resolving to give an apology for a friendly conversation that became unfriendly, working through sadness to harvest organs from a six-year-old child, or knowing God is available in all situations, even working through secular messages. It's a must read for those who, like myself, want to experience Jesus on a deeper level.

—Laurel Jean Becker, speaker and author of *Tales from Weaver Pond* and *In the Heart of a Quiet Garden*

(www.laureljeanbecker.com)

Laura's storytelling is like a potato chip: you cannot stop at one. I was compelled to read one after the other, I simply could not get enough of the delicious story after story falling from her lips—pure goodness for your soul!

— Rev. Dr. Dan Dolquist

What if we all could view life through the eyes of Jesus? What if we could truly see the love of God and His mercy and grace in everyday situations and circumstances that continually surround us? In *Jesus in Shorts*, author Laura Padgett invites us to come outside of ourselves and see our lives, our situations and circumstances, in a more excellent manner than we ever have before. She invites readers to fully grasp life the way God wants us to grasp life, so we can see that there is so much more than what our physical eyes can see. Laura Padgett is one of God's writing vessels for such a time as this—for His glory and for our edification.

—Beatrice Bruno, US Army veteran, speaker, and author of *The Baby Chronicles: Where You Were Before You Were* (www.DrillSergeantofLife.com)

When a writer, author, and storyteller unselfishly shares her transforming spiritual experiences on the page with humility, humanity, honesty, and integrity, the reader can't help but be blessed. This is "*Jesus in Shorts*" and, Laura Padgett. And I'm Blessed!

— Stephen Ray Watts, musician and songwriter, Dotsero® Praise Fellowship™

Laura Padgett's *Jesus in Shorts* is a marvelous book of short stories. Whether reading about a surgical technician, a new fisherman, or a Christmas elf, I was delighted. Laura's compassion, humor and sweetness paint moments in vivid color. *Jesus in Shorts* is the kind of book you want to read while you're relaxing in sweet sunshine or snuggling in a blanket by a warm fire. Wonderful!

— Robbie Iobst, author of *Cecelia Jackson's Last Chance*

Julia,

May God bless you as you travel with Him.

Nancy 2018

Feb 29·18

JESUS IN SHORTS

Twenty-five Short Stories of Life-Changing Jesus Moments

by
Laura L. Padgett, M.A.

Illustrations by
Sally M. Cordrey

JESUS IN SHORTS

Illumify Media Global
www.IllumifyMedia.com
"Write. Market. Publish. SELL!"

Illustrations by Sally M. Cordrey (sally.cordrey@gmail.com)
used with permission.

Paperback ISBN: 978-1-947360-11-2
eBook ISBN: 978-1-947360-12-9

This book is dedicated to Albert and Audrey Carvallo, my parents who were the first, and best, storytellers in my world. Whether Papa told stories about working on the Rio Grande Railroad in Grand Junction, Colorado or Mama chronicled the antics of her rogue cat, their colorful (and sometimes comical) tales provided hours of entertainment for my sisters, our friends, and me. Every time I write, dance or speak a story, I am reminded of their examples and grateful for this gift they passed to me.

CONTENTS

Acknowledgments

I CANNOT IMAGINE COMPLETING a project of this magnitude without the wise counsel of the man God sent to be my helpmate, protector of dreams, and tireless cheerleader. My husband, Keith, pulls me off my pity pot, gives me solid advice, prays with and for me, and loves me when I am unlovable. He believes in me when I stop believing in myself. In his eyes I see the woman I want to be.

The illustrations by my talented and generous friend Sally Cordrey have added valuable visuals to each piece in this book. Her patience with me as I attempted to explain my visions was inexhaustible and I appreciate her work, time, and most of all her friendship.

I am indebted to my friend and fellow writer Royalene Doyle for her first editing of this manuscript. She helped me get it ready for further editing and formatting.

My photographer, Sandee Flanagan, helped me present just the right image on my author bio. She worked to ensure we had quality photos that were taken in the place I love most in the world—Golden, Colorado.

There is never just one voice that goes into a project like this. My beta readers brought fresh, authentic, and interesting perspectives to each tale. To Joyce and Jim Little, Laura Pierce, Lori Marcello, Sandee Flanagan, Kathy Cagg, and Heather Pearce, I say, "Thank you faithful and honest friends."

I am grateful to my friends who offered the foreword and written endorsements for this collection of stories. To be in the company of such talented and accomplished artists is a blessing. To have their approval and encouragement is humbling.

FOREWORD
Come. Sip. Savor.

MY FRIEND LAURA HAS poured the wine and broken the bread. These stories are communion. An offering that invites us to experience the ever-present God who dwells within our souls just as fully as He dwells in a grand, stained-glass cathedral or a little, white clapboard church on a dusty prairie. This God walks with us in our normal, everyday lives as completely as He walked with King David, Martin Luther King Jr., or the Apostle Paul.

Ours is a God who notices everything. About the world. About us. He enjoys our delight as we pause to breathe in a sunset.

He feels our pain when our tender places are bumped. He holds our dreams close to His heart. He is the Friend who laughs and weeps with us, the Savior who sacrifices all for us, the Defender who fights for us.

As the stories in *Jesus in Shorts* illustrate, our God tenderly cultivates our heart. He speaks to our longings, our fears, our hopes, and futures. He sends the voices of the clarity, encouragement, and wisdom we need.

He *blesses* us.

Our God never falters as He steps out with us on our individual journeys. He goes before and waits in our future. He walks beside in our present, simultaneously on our right and on our left. He comes behind us, protecting the good work He has already done and opening our hearts to heal as we process our past. He surrounds us with goodness and grace.

The Lord, our Shepherd, leads us to quiet places of repose—green grass, still waters. It is here He brings soul rest, the kind that slips to our deepest places and ever-so-gently kneads away the knots. He releases the pain, the fear, and the questions. We are restored.

This Jesus makes us brave. Better. Stronger. Kinder. Wiser.

This Jesus is who Laura reveals in the following pages. They don't simply tell sweet stories, they unwrap God-moments, showing us who He is and how He lives with us.

With beauty, humor, and insight Laura illustrates this glorious journey with Jesus, celebrating poignant moments that are both rare and ordinary. It's like Jesus to take a normal day and give it extraordinary grace.

Come. Sip. Savor.

Linger.

These stories are not to be rushed through; though they are so engaging you'll be tempted.

They are hidden treasures revealed. Breathe. Pause. Partake.

Jesus will meet you here.

— Paula Moldenhauer,
author of the *Soul Scents* devotional book series

Introduction

WHAT IS THE PURPOSE of aging if not to gain wisdom from life's trials and triumphs? What purpose is there in gaining wisdom unless we choose to share it with others? Is it possible to see diminished physical beauty (according to the world's view) as a secondary consideration when we realize we have the most beautiful gift of all in the form of wisdom (according to God's view) achieved by growing older?

These were questions some friends and I pondered one morning as we lifted our lattes in salute to the youngest member of our group while she showed us her newly minted Medicare card. I personally had no trouble sharing my views on the questions because I was blessed in my mid-twenties by a relationship with the most beautiful and wise person I ever met. Her name was Dolores. She lived to be over one hundred years old. Our relationship lasted for thirty-five years.

Dolores taught me God defines beauty at every age and every stage. He honors wisdom gained by living life, experiencing failure, enjoying success, and learning lessons found in God's own classrooms. She also taught me that sharing His wisdom with others multiplies the blessings to the giver and the one(s) gifted. We are not to hold onto what we gain or are gifted with in life.

Sometimes in writer's groups I hear people say they have been writing their whole lives. Or that they always wanted to be writers. These statements do not describe my journey as an author. My favorite art is dance. I always thought that telling a story orally or in movement was, for me, more effective than writing it. Then God showed me His plan for my retirement years included a transformation of that mind-set.

As a child of a Sicilian father and Scots-Irish mother, there was no shortage of storytelling around our house. I sat many nights and heard my father weave tales that mesmerized all who listened to him. Some he made up. Some he told from life experiences. It was the same with my Celtic mother. Eventually, I began expressing myself in the same way to entertain, educate, and inspire others.

When I went to graduate school, it was no surprise to anyone that I took writing classes to refine my storytelling, and then declared a major in storytelling through movement. I found that a pencil gliding on paper or keys clicking on my computer were other forms of dancing my stories.

God called me to write and publish my first book, *Dolores, Like the River,* in 2013. It was then that I realized I can have two forms of expression that flow, move, and dance together. I was changed in the process of writing that book into an artist who now sees the written story has tremendous power to inspire, encourage, and help others transform and grow.

Since that time, I have been published in various short-story anthologies like *Chicken Soup for the Soul: Merry Christmas* and *Chicken Soup for the Soul: Think Possible* as well as *Letters To America* by Xulon Press. The stories that were published in those books are included in this assortment.

This book details some of my encounters with Jesus Christ, my Lord and Savior, as He has taken care of, taught, and mentored me for over six decades. While writing these stories, I was again reminded of God's faithful attendance to me as a treasured child, even before I knew Him.

Reflected here is only a small fraction of the lessons I have learned on my journey of sixty-seven years in my earthly temple. There are hundreds more for me as there are for anyone, regardless of age. Each account I share has been prayed over in an attempt to determine the messages God wants imparted. In honor of my wise earthly mentor, Dolores, and out of obedience to a God who expects us to share the gifts He has given, I offer these tales of life, learning, searching, and gratitude for His faithful care.

If you dread getting older or find no possible value in the process, I pray you will consider looking through a new lens when examining the purpose of aging. I encourage you to view the wisdom you have received with a grateful heart and embrace willingness to pass along the lessons learned. It is my hope that you will find gratitude for what He has done for you and maybe even inspiration to share that with others in a world that desperately needs Christ and the hope of His message today.

If you like these stories, please visit my website at lauralpadgett.com and click on the link to my blog, "Livin' What You're Given." I would be honored if you share my blog or books with others of any generation.

CHAPTER 1

Can't Talk to a Numb Tongue

*See to it, brothers and sisters, that none of you
has a sinful, unbelieving heart that turns away
from the living God. But encourage one another
daily, as long as it is called "Today," so that none
of you may be hardened by sin's deceitfulness.*
—Hebrews 3:12-13

FOR ALL WHO CHERISH THEIR FRIENDS
ENOUGH TO SAY AND ACCEPT, "I'M SORRY"

I WASN'T SURE WHAT was more oppressive,
my fear of dental work as I sat in the chair for
my appointment or my sense of guilt at the way

1

a disagreement with a friend ended the previous evening. That conversation weighed heavily on my mind. We were talking politics. This friend and I have been on opposite sides of most issues for more than thirty years. In the past, we have always been open to different points of view and kept civility in our conversations. This is due, in large part, to our mutual love for the Lord Jesus Christ.

Our conversation began calmly. But before long we were talking over each other, insisting only one person could be right; and we ended just this side of exchanging personal potshots. Anyone who has taken a debate class knows your argument is lost as soon as you resort to insulting your opponent because it screams, "My position is weak as water, and the only way I can win is to distract you with put-downs."

Still, passion is passion and it doesn't always provide an exit ramp from the highway of self-righteousness. What's worse, the unshakable posture "I'm right" will push us full speed past the line of protecting dignity—ours or another's.

I was pulled from my guilt-filled musings when my dentist (a fellow I like very much) came to deliver that always pleasant shot in the jaw from a needle that feels like it's the size of a garden hose. During the injection I did my usual routine: remembered breathing techniques learned in childbirth classes, tried not to lose control of any bodily functions and prayed really, really hard.

After half my face and tongue felt dead, the hygienist began prep work. This process was complicated by my inability to get my tongue out of the way. I tried complying with her request to pull the pesky organ aside. But it simply was not a manageable task. I tried to apologize with words. That, too, was not manageable. I looked up helplessly. The hygienist laughed and said,

"I know you're trying, Hon. But it's hard to talk to a numb tongue."

I attempted a nod and smile. Instead I sort of just blinked and drooled at her. She patted my hand and together with the dentist we shared the space for an hour until they completed the procedure.

When I returned home, I sat down with my Bible, which I hadn't had time to read prior to starting the day's activities. I turned to the Scripture passage of the day in my favorite devotional: "But no human being can tame the tongue. It is a restless evil, full of deadly poison" (James 3:8).

I squirmed in my chair when I realized God was talking to me about the previous day's conflict. It was not only what I said, but how I said it. My tongue was untamed and unruly because my ego got in the way. I was so bent on being right, I didn't stop to consider that my words, and tone, were hurtful.

I mused about this, pouted a little and did the familiar three-year-old mental shifting from one foot to the other while pleading, "She started it, God. And besides look how everyone is acting right now. We are just so uptight and steeped in unkindness. What do You expect when we live in this world You gave us?"

I knew in my heart this wasn't going to fly with the Almighty any more than Adam pointing a finger and saying, "Yeah, well it's all her fault," got him off the hook for the transgression that led to the Eden eviction.

God makes it very clear that no matter how others act, we are responsible for our own behavior. His kids are called to act differently, period. If there was a problem with my friend, He would deal with that. It was not my business.

After some time on the pity pot, I climbed onto my Father's lap and asked Him to forgive me. I told him I would call the other party and ask her forgiveness too, when I could manage to get words out without slurring them.

As the Novocain wore off, I was in a considerable amount of pain. The discomfort was not from the dental work itself, but from where I bit my tongue when I couldn't feel it. The Holy One was nudging me.

I sat back in my chair trying to ignore my throbbing tongue and shared a giggle (sort of) with God. "Oh, I see. When the tongue is numb it can cause great harm, to me and to others. That's the poisonous part you talk about in James, right? Okay, I get it, Lord."

The next day I called my friend and offered an apology for my insensitivity. She accepted and offered one of her own. We agreed to be more mindful of how we communicate in the future. We agreed that we are never called, as believers, to be silent on important issues.

Regardless of belief systems, we still have an obligation to govern our democracy, which is made more difficult if we refuse to learn from others and engage in respectful dialogue because of our own rigid stances.

While neither of us changed the other's mind, we prayed over the phone and came away reaffirmed that relationships are more important than what one person perceives as right or wrong. After a lengthy conversation, we planned to meet for lunch the next week.

I hung up and returning to James 3:8, I asked God to help me remember this lesson. He assured me that Scripture, when taken to heart, proves to be the best practice for walking this world. God's Word helps me speak my truth in love, lend my voice to important issues, and respect *and* learn from other voices. But most of all, it provides a solid model for loving by leading my conversations without a numb tongue.

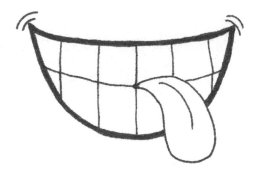

Reflection Notes

Sometimes competition can throw us into a "win at all costs" mind-set. But that is not God's way. He wants us to live in peace and harmony. In dialogue with others, we will not always agree. But there are ways to disagree that do not sacrifice our dignity and grieve the Holy Spirit. Have you harshly criticized someone? Have you made amends for that? Maybe it's time to set that right. Or maybe it's time to accept the amends from another if they have been harsh in their response to you.

CHAPTER 2

Silver and Gold

*"Always go with your passions. Never ask yourself
if it is realistic or not."*
—Deepak Chopra

For Michelle Farrell, Judy Denapoli,
and Sally Cordrey

Sunlight streamed through the holes in
the tent roof. It bathed the gold medal I held,
making it appear almost liquid in my sweating
palm. I earned the medal for performing the
hornpipe, a difficult solo step, at an Irish step
dance competition. The sun's rays warmed my

body on that cold September day in Estes Park, Colorado. There was no need, however, for an external heating source to warm my soul. The happiness and pride I felt flowed from my heart to my mouth, producing a grin like that on a small child's face while unwrapping Christmas presents.

I wanted to enjoy the moment forever, determined never to forget what it took to get to the top of the podium. The odds were long for a woman in her fifties to win the trophy. I thanked God for the realization of this dream and knew my health and strength depended, in large part, upon Him.

Even though I was delighted, I couldn't help recalling the discouragement and laughter from some of my close friends when I told them of my plans to learn Irish dance. Their remarks stung at first. Then I chose to see their unkindness as a gauntlet thrown down at my feet. I decided to pick up that gauntlet and run, actually dance, with it. Still their lack of support left me questioning why God gave me a desire and then peppered my life with friends who openly expressed discouragement and doubts.

When I discovered my passion for Irish dance in my mid-forties, I sought resources for learning everything I could about it. I took classes, practiced every day, paid for private lessons, went to workshops, and listened nonstop to music for competitions and shows. I never liked competitions. But, they forced me to practice and elevate my technical skills. Over the years, I accumulated a few silver and bronze medals. And that bright day in Colorado I held the gold.

Medals are a source of pride for me. They validate my hard work. But on that particular occasion, winning a medal also provided an avenue for learning a valuable lesson about art and heart.

At the end of the contest, while I stood in the dancer's tent admiring my medal, a pair of hard-soled dance shoes flew past my head. The angry competitor didn't aim her shoes in my direction, but she did aim her angry words at me. "You have no right to that medal, Padgett. You're way too old to be dancing, competing, or even thinking about performing an art this demanding and athletic. Even if you were an appropriate age to enter this level of competition, I should have won. I'm much better at technique, timing, and all-around dancing than you will ever be," she blurted out. She exited the tent, leaving me staring after her in disbelief.

I didn't know what to say or feel. I heard all the words of those who mocked my little dream resurrected and flung at me through an invisible, high-powered sound system. While trying to regain my emotional balance I felt a hand rest on my right shoulder. An unfamiliar voice with an Irish lilt whispered, "Do you believe her?"

I turned to face the judge who moments ago awarded me the gold. "Yes ma'am. She has better technique and sense of musical timing. She is just all around better than me."

"No, she isn't. Do you know the difference between the silver and gold? Do you know why you were awarded this medal today?" Her voice was barely audible against the sound of self-condemnation in my mind that was feeding a feeling of foolishness.

I dropped my gaze and shook my head.

She lifted my chin and looked into my teary eyes. "You reflected hours of practice and honing of your craft, just like many others. You kept the beat and executed a difficult step, like many others. Your posture was straight, and you demonstrated ability to remember the intricacies required. You were up against some tough competitors out there today, and you gave a flawless performance. From a judge's point of view, it can be difficult to select one dancer over another when awarding medals.

"But if mechanics and technical merit are equal, the decision will fall to the one who dances with heart. Some *do* the dance; others *are* the dance. Today, you *were* the dance. And that, my friend, is gold."

That was my last Irish dance competition, not because I feared being struck in the head by airborne footwear but because the calendar does not lie. I was not getting any younger. My years of hard, competitive Irish dancing were over.

I'm not prone to melancholy over things out of my control—like the passage of time that brings aging of body and mind. And I honestly cannot say I spend time looking at dance medals I've collected. There are not many uses for my little treasures beyond evoking smiles from a face sporting wrinkles fashioned by determination.

Still, I have found the medals do prove beneficial once in a while. For example, when I see someone about to let a dream slip away because of age, perceived inabilities, or opinions of critics, I extend an invitation. "Would you come to my house for tea, please? I want to show you something."

Reflection Notes

Why do we often give weight to critics over the voices of our hearts and the God who loves us beyond all measure? Have you ever succumbed to negative influences encouraging you to drop a dream or desire? Ask God today if that is something He wants you to revisit. With Him you can grasp that dream. If He has helped you realize a dream or desire, say "Thank you," right now, today.

CHAPTER 3

"It's for Everyone"

"They say a person needs just three things to be truly happy in this world: someone to love, something to do, and something to hope for."
—Tom Bodett

FOR THE LATE WARREN (SANTA CLAUS) HOWARD

ONE WOULD THINK A seasoned member of Santa's helpers, and captain of the Golden, Colorado, elves, could answer any Christmas-related question thrown her way. However, that was not the case this time. My inability to construct, let alone articulate, an answer was not because it was a difficult question. It was due to the setting, and what appeared to be the reason, behind the child's query.

A few years ago, at Christmastime, my lieutenant elves and I were helping Santa in a church-based homeless shelter. We were attempting to keep the excited children in line while awaiting their one-on-one time with St. Nick. I was distracted from my duties by a tug at the bottom of my red and green tunic. A young boy, whose head came only to the middle of my five-foot frame, stood looking up at me. His twinkling brown eyes and wide, gap-toothed grin greeted me. He motioned for me to bring an elf ear closer to his mouth.

"Miss Elf, is Christmas for me too this year?"

His expectant expression punctured my soul. I was taken by surprise and trying to understand his need for clarification on this issue. I slowly raised up, hoping to buy time to come up with an appropriate answer. Somehow, a simple "yes" just didn't seem to be enough.

"Yes. Yes, sweetest child," I said. "Christmas is for everyone. And it's especially for you this year."

The twinkle in his eyes grew brighter as he received the answer. He nodded his head as if I had confirmed what he already knew and then moved in the direction of the big guy in red.

I was pretty sure there was a twinkle in my eyes as well. But my glimmer was due to tears bubbling up from a heart stung by his simple, sad question. I wondered how many times he had asked that question and what answers he may have received.

The boy and Santa were soon engaged in quiet, animated conversation. I couldn't take my eyes off of him until I heard a soft voice in my left ear, "Thank you. May I give you a hug?"

I turned to face a woman in perhaps her mid-twenties. Her eyes were as misty as mine, but she was smiling much like the young man I had spoken with a few seconds earlier. Their similarities were unmistakable. I smiled and nodded my head. Her arms wrapped around me before I could blink. Then stepping back, she asked permission to tell me her story. I nodded again.

Her hand rested on my red, velvet-clad arm. "These last four years, my two children and I have lived on the streets after I ran from an abusive relationship, trying to keep us safe. In summer months we sleep under bridges. In winter we're housed overnight in shelters, when there's room for us."

She dropped her head as she continued. "I never completed high school, you see. So I've only been able to find temporary and part-time work."

When she looked back up, a smile accompanied the rest of her tale. "After I passed my GED a few weeks ago, I was accepted into a training program for a career I think will provide a livable income for us. This is the first real Christmas my children will remember. And at last I see light at the end of what has been a dark road for us. I have hope now for a brighter future. For the first time in years, I believe we will be okay."

As she shared her journey, I gained an understanding into why her son asked the question. Having wrapped up his conference with Santa, her young child joined her. They moved to a table spread with roasted turkeys, hams, sweet potatoes, and a variety of freshly baked pies. The little guy pulled his mother toward the celebratory feast then stopped and turned to look at me. I smiled and winked at him. He smiled back, waved, and attempted a wink by blinking both eyes twice.

I left the church that night with elf bells jingling and pointed green shoes plodding along in a snow-covered parking lot. I thanked God for His mercies and for that little family. I felt gratitude for being able to witness that moment in their transitional season.

As I considered what had happened, I asked myself if I had ever really understood the true meaning of Christmas before then. Had I ever been such a close witness to hope offered to the hopeless? Had I ever really taken time from my busy schedule to observe others experiencing new life and another chance? Wasn't that really what Christmas was supposed to be about?

While sitting in my car, under a city street light, I watched the snowflakes fall upon my windshield. I mulled over the numerous times

I'd celebrated in decorated churches, sang carols, opened presents, and enjoyed delicious food. Yet, I could not remember ever feeling the peace and joy I unwrapped that night as I answered the simple question of a child who knows homelessness and street life firsthand but refuses to relinquish his precious sense of hopefulness.

I can honestly testify that in an old church, on a wintery Denver night, in the presence of a child-angel who relied on a secular elf to answer a sacred question, I was the recipient of the true Christmas blessing. I understood that every year, in the busyness of the worldly holiday season, there is one question that must never go unanswered: "Is the true promise of Christmas for *me* too this year?"

Reflection Notes

Do you take time in your day to see our Lord in the faces of strangers, especially those who have fallen on difficult times? Can you take a few minutes today to notice our Savior in the eyes, expressions, stories, and even circumstances of others?

CHAPTER 4

Vehicle for Change

"It is no use walking anywhere to preach unless our walking is our preaching."
—St. Francis of Assisi

FOR LYNARD, THE PEACEMAKER

I WAS SITTING IN MY car, enjoying the view of swaying wild grasses, singing trees, and a lake filled to the brim at Crown Hill Park near Denver. Before I could get out and begin my walk around the water, a man approached me. This is a common occurrence when I drive my gem from the sixties, and I'm accustomed to total strangers starting conversations about my car. Mostly these are pleasant encounters. This particular gentleman wore a hat displaying the name of a politician I didn't support. Because of some past experiences, I braced for another personal attack because of my foreign car. My defenses fell away when he flashed an exuberant smile.

"Wow, what a beautiful old VW Beetle. What year is it?" He asked, looking at my car, Lynard, and not at me. I was looking at him and not his hat.

"He's a '69 model."

"No kidding. I had a '68 just like it. My brother and I took a cross-country trip in that little car. We had some good times. I love these old jalopies. Every time I see one, I think of my brother. He went to Nam after high school; he never came home." He looked toward the water, and we fell silent as we shared common grief from a time of great loss in our youth.

"I've always wanted to buy another car like this, but my wife thinks it's too extravagant. She doesn't understand 'Beetle Fever'."

I nodded. "I know the feeling. Of all the cars I've ever owned, Lynard is fender and hood above the rest."

"Why did you name him Lynard?" He stopped calling Lynard "it" and used the pronoun "him."

"He's named after Lynyrd Skynyrd. The spelling is different but somehow nothing else seemed to fit him." His grin told me he recognized the 1970's rock band. This time he nodded.

"Well, that's a fine name for this guy. You two have a good day. I have to get my daily walk in before it gets too warm. Take care of yourself, and that car. He's a treasure."

I assured him that Lynard was in the best of hands as he and his dog moved toward the walking path around the lake. I leaned my head on the headrest, closed my eyes, thanked God I met a new person and that Lynard brought a smile, and sense of camaraderie, to the stranger and me. I asked forgiveness for my rush to judgment because of past wounds that had nothing to do with this man.

When I opened my eyes, there was a woman waving at me and coming toward my car. I was trying to figure out if I knew her as she came to the driver's side and asked, "How old is your car?"

"He's a '69."

"I graduated from high school in 1967, and I remember these cars. I had one just like him. She was my constant companion. Why do you call your car him?" she asked, continuing to admire Lynard from bumper to bumper.

"He's named after Lynyrd Skynyrd. I'm an old hippie, and Lynard is a free bird."

She clapped her hands and issued a deep, throaty laugh as she tilted her head skyward.

Sunshine danced off her silver crown. "I saw that band in 1973. The song 'Free Bird' is one of a kind. What a great guitar solo in that one. I've never heard anything like it since. Our generation had the best music, don't you agree?"

"Yes ma'am."

"You know," she said, "my father's name was Leonard. He passed away almost fifteen years ago. I still miss him most days. I think you and I were meant to meet today. I'm Lorraine." She extended her hand.

"I'm Laura and this, as you know, is Lynard." I took her hand in mine. We didn't hurry to let go of one another.

She stroked the top of my car as if touching the face of a baby. "I bet you get lots of attention with this car."

"Well, it's not so much about the attention. It's about making folks smile. You see, I believe we live in a world that's toxic like never before. It seems we are all at each other with anger, fear, suspicion, and attempted division. I'm not innocent in all these behaviors either. So Lynard and I are on a mission of sorts. We roll around trying to find common ground and connections with others. He brings lots of smiles and memories. Everyone has a VW Bug tale. I feel like, in a small way, my little car helps heal the brokenness in me and our world through shared stories."

"Well he does that for sure. I couldn't agree with you more about this world. We have to get back to loving, or at least liking, each other. God bless you, my new friend. And God bless you too, Lynard."

She took her leave and walked to her own vehicle. I tapped Lynard's steering wheel and said, "Old man, you are something else. Who says God can use only humans to do His work of spreading joy and unity? You be good and try to keep people smiling while I go for my walk, okay?"

I got out of Lynard, locked his doors, and headed for my stroll by the water. Before I ventured more than a few yards, I noticed a young lady sitting on a bench near the walking path. She was putting on a pair of roller skates that were white with pink-rimmed wheels, high top laces and toe-stops.

"Hello," I greeted her.

"Hello."

"You know," I told her, "I used to have some skates just like that. Those bring back great memories of my youth."

She beamed at me and said she couldn't help noticing my car. "I love those cars. My granddad used to have one. How old is yours?"

Reflection Notes

We live in a country and world that promotes division along religious, political, gender, and racial lines. Where has God called you to walk the ministry of Christ by promoting unity? How do you see that working for your life—in your family, community, and the world?

CHAPTER 5

Mama's Ring

"Compassion brings us to a stop, and for a moment we rise above ourselves."
—Mason Cooley

❧

FOR MAMA

WHEN YOU LOOK AT me, you would never guess my mother had the green eyes and red hair most people associate with Scots-Irish ethnicity. With dark hair and brown eyes, I resemble my Sicilian father. If Mama was happy, her eyes sparkled like green gems flirting with sunlight; and she was a joyful spirit dancing without care. I loved watching those eyes twinkle, especially when she told her stories of ballroom dancing.

You also would never know that behind the sparkle of Mama's eyes, lay pain authored by the disease of alcoholism. Her illness became so severe that she estranged herself from her three daughters for the last ten years of her life. She never met her only grandson, Gabriel, my boy. It would be a lie to say I did not resent her illness, and her choices.

After her death, I received a box containing her belongings. Among those was her wedding ring. It was in need of major repair if it was to be worn again. I wasn't sure it was worth the bother and wondered why God allowed such a painful reminder to catch up to me. I saw the ring as a symbol of all that was wrong with my mother, our family, and my childhood. It was broken, tarnished, and represented the brutal dysfunction framing memories of my early years. But for some reason, I yearned to have this ring repaired and to wear it.

When I took the ring to a local jeweler, he promised to do his best to fix it but confessed, "Frankly, it's probably too broken to be restored."

This statement reflected how I saw my mother and our relationship. I agreed to leave it and accepted that because it was close to Valentine's Day, his busiest time of the year, he couldn't get to it for a few weeks.

The next month, he called and said the ring was repaired and ready to collect. I arrived at his shop and found him admiring my mother's ring. He called me over to inspect it. I couldn't believe the difference. The gold glimmered and the diamond, held in place with new tines, sparkled as it flirted with sunlight coming from a nearby window. I knew then why God wanted me to have, and wear, this ring.

I had some choices to make. I could hold onto an image of my mother as a tarnished, weak and broken woman who neglected her girls because of alcohol. Or I could remember her sparkle and shine, and those amazing eyes. I could choose to acknowledge the good things Mama gave me.

These thoughts reminded me that we are all broken. Yet Jesus sees through that brokenness and counts us as flawless gems. He tells us that only through forgiveness are we healed and free.

The jeweler spoke in a low voice. "It's quite a beauty, isn't it?"

"Yes. Yes, she was," I said placing the ring on my finger and making my choice.

"I'm sorry it took so long to get it to you," he apologized.

"That's okay. You see today, March 9, would've been my mother's eighty-third birthday."

We stood in silence for a moment before he moved away to help another customer. While they engaged in conversation, I began speaking to the woman who birthed me as if she stood at my side.

"Happy birthday, Mama. I love you. I forgive you. Please forgive me. Much of what I am today, and what I have, is because I inherited many gifts from you. Thank you."

When I spoke those last two words, a cold block of resentment in my heart broke and began thawing. I relaxed into peace fueled by gratitude for God's gentle, persistent teaching about the value of appreciation and forgiveness. For the first time, I saw my mother's decisions had resulted from a struggle causing more pain and isolation for her than for anyone. My tears flowed as I imagined what her life must really have been like.

I stood outside the jewelry shop, in a warm Colorado spring wind, and counted just some of the gifts my mother gave me, including a quick wit, a keen sense of humor, and most of all the ability and desire to dance. I allowed the full weight of loss to fall on me as I realized I never truly knew the person Mama was because of a disease that destroyed her relationships.

I wear this ring frequently to honor my mother and to remember her happy, sparkling, green eyes and free spirit. It reminds me that harboring resentment brings nothing but harm to us on a frequent basis; but gratitude and forgiveness provide benefits for our whole lives. Although I still battle memories from my childhood, God is teaching me how processing pain through the lens of compassion can dissolve bitterness.

When I transition to my eternal home beyond earth, Mama's ring is willed to my granddaughter Sophia. It is my prayer she will live a life filled with gratitude for her gifts and the gifts of others. I also pray she will focus on the sparkle and shine all around her; and that she will never see herself or others as too broken to be restored.

Reflection Notes

Is there a person you need to forgive? If so, ask God to help you find a way to feel compassion, even for one who may have hurt you. He will help you do that. If you need to ask forgiveness, God will help you do that too. You may find one will lead to the other.

CHAPTER 6

Fresh Hair

"Smile, breathe and go slowly."
—Thich Nhat Hanh

❧

FOR ALL WHO CANNOT FIND TIME TO SLOW
DOWN

THE LAST THING I do before I leave my house for any activity, is apply hairspray on my unruly locks in an attempt to make them behave. This is vital when you consider I live in a state where wind gusts can reach better than fifty miles per hour and can make my hair look like a creation from a food processor. Although

I don't spend enormous amounts of time on makeup and hair each day (ten minutes is my max), I try to honor my mother's request that her girls never leave the house without looking "put together."

Like most people with busy schedules, I often multitask. It's not uncommon for me to use my grooming time to mentally inventory the planned events of the day. Some days it feels I have more obligations than could be considered manageable. It's easy for me to create such a hectic schedule that I am literally crashing into myself as I progress from task to task. In the past, I have falsely believed that if I mentally organize every little detail, I can prevent derailment from unexpected inconveniences.

Each New Year I resolve to reduce my stress by managing my time better and slowing down so I'm not always dashing around like an athlete trying to beat an Olympic record. Sometimes

I'm successful, physically. But slowing my mind to less than warp speed has proven to be more difficult.

As I put myself together one day, prior to leaving for a book signing event, I noticed the scent of bathroom air freshener was particularly strong. The antiseptic fragrance followed me into the kitchen.

While grabbing my handbag, I complained to Keith that our current air freshener was overpowering, and we would have to change brands. To my horror, he sniffed in my direction and smiled. My eyes popped wide open as I heard what he was not saying.

Without delay, I dashed to the bathroom, jerked open the vanity cupboard door and stared at the air freshener sitting right next to the hairspray. Apparently, I had, in fact, given my black and silver crown a healthy coating of Lysol.

I moaned. "Oh, that's all I need. There's no time to wash and style my hair now."

As I performed a sort of mental foot stomping, I was overtaken with laughter. I stopped my moaning and just let the humor of the situation roll over me. What a great lesson God gave me in the art of truly pacing myself.

On the bright side, the Lysol made my gray hair shine. And no doubt I was protected from any germ that dared venture into Jefferson County. But sporting air freshener to a public event is not my first grooming choice. I could blame the incident on getting older (being more forgetful) or on putting the hairspray and Lysol too close together in the cupboard. Distractions are part of life, and I am not going to pretend I'll ever be a poster child for intentional mindfulness. But I couldn't help admitting that the busier I get, the more potential I have for making mistakes. After having a good laugh, I had to admit the truth. I need to slow down, relax, and take things a little easier all around. It is not enough to slow my body down. I must pay attention to the pace of the little gray cells too.

Keith and I processed the incident and decided we were just caught up in the rush, rush, rush that represents the world we live in. Together we offered God a prayer of thanksgiving for the lesson learned about the high cost of being distanced from the here and now.

During prayer time the next morning, I asked God to help me. "Please, Lord," I petitioned, "heighten my awareness of when I'm moving from serenity and into a frantic pace that may author mistakes causing inconvenience for me and others. Some days I need help focusing less on schedules, obligation, and demands, as I op for mindfulness."

After leaving my prayer room, I took a few minutes to rearrange the bathroom vanity cupboard. I know I can count on God to help me be more attentive, but I also thought it wouldn't hurt to do a little of my own leg work in order to assure future Lysol-free hair.

Reflection Notes

Do you ever feel that life's demands and your attempts to respond to them leave you running on the proverbial hamster wheel? Ask God today to show you how and where you can make time to just be in His presence and breathe. Perhaps in your time with Him, He will show you areas where you can enjoy life more by practicing mindfulness and simplicity.

CHAPTER 7

Thelma's Blessing

In His hand is the life of every creature and the
breath of all mankind.

—Job 12:10

FOR THELMA PADGETT, 1920-2014

IT HAS BEEN SEVERAL years since my mother-
in-law went home to the Lord. During the
last ten years of her life, Thelma suffered from
the debilitating effects of Parkinson's disease,
with tremors and memory loss. When she
approached the end stage of her disease, it was
sometimes difficult for her to settle into rest.

At those times, she took great comfort in having her caretaker, or one of her family members, read to her from the well-worn Bible she kept at her bedside. She was fond of a certain devotional magazine as well. Reading from that publication, along with Scripture, afforded Thelma the opportunity to discuss applications of God's word in her life and, sometimes, in ours.

One Saturday several weeks prior to her death, my husband and I visited Thelma in her Oklahoma home. Our visits with her were always special. But this time with her was made even more memorable by the presence of our great-niece, one of Thelma's great-granddaughters, Abigail.

For that night's devotional time, Thelma (Mom) asked those family members present to be at her bedside and take turns reading parts of the Scripture and devotional message. My sister-in-law, Deana, my husband, Keith,

Abigail, and I formed a circle around her bed. We held hands and did as she requested. At the beginning of the reading, Thelma's hands shook as she picked at the bed clothing.

We started by reading the Scripture verse: "In his hand is the life of every creature and the breath of all mankind" (Job 12:10).

She gazed at each family member as we took our turn reading the devotional. As we read to her, Thelma's tremors and clutching of the bed clothes ceased. I looked at her now calm face and wondered if Thelma thought she might be gazing upon some of us for the last time on this side of the Kingdom. At the conclusion of the reading, she closed her eyes and began taking deep breaths. We thought she had fallen asleep.

When we moved away from the bedside, she raised her hands out in front of her. Again, I was struck by the absence of tremors. She opened her eyes and said, "God bless my family near and far. Please be with each one and keep them safe."

Only after invoking God's favor for her loved ones, did she drift into sleep. Standing next to my great-niece, I whispered, "Child, be here in the moment. Do not allow your mind to wander. You have received a blessing from the matriarch of our family. There are few things as precious as what you've been part of tonight. Be in this moment, Abby; be bathed by it, and hold it forever."

On January 2, 2014, Thelma stepped over the threshold of human life and into the light and love of her eternal home. She departed less than two months after what turned out to be our final visit with her. At her funeral, the family requested this same Scripture verse be read. I sat between my husband and my sister-in-law, and we held hands. I reflected on that night and the beautiful presence of a woman who believed that, indeed, God is in charge of our living, and our dying.

While Pastor Sharon read the words at the memorial service in Prairie Chapel—a church Thelma attended most of her life, baptized her children in, and buried her husband and one son in—I was flooded with gratitude. I thanked God for the night, and moment, we stood around the bed of our precious family elder and received her blessing.

Then I whispered, "Thank you, Mom, for one of the most meaningful memories I will ever hold. Our last visit with you was sweet. But knowing you are in the presence of our Lord is sweeter still. Bless you dearest lady on this, your final journey."

Reflection Notes

In a culture that honors all things youthful and often labels older people as being in the way, do you ever take time to appreciate the elders in your family, church, community? If not, you're missing some of life's richest blessings and most valuable lessons. Have a look at those older than you through a new light. Maybe spend some time with aging family members or elderly people in your church and community. The lifelong blessings will add to the rich experiences of your life.

CHAPTER 8

Exactly as Instructed

"A good laugh overcomes more difficulties and dissipates more dark clouds than any other one thing."
—Laura Ingalls Wilder

FOR GABE
AND DOLORES

"THESE YEARS DON'T LAST forever. When you look back, you'll see I am right about that." These words came from my friend and mentor, Dolores, when my small son and I were visiting her one afternoon.

Dolores' children were grown and living their own lives when I met her. She taught hundreds of young people as an educator, prior to retiring. She was my "go-to" person for advice on how to parent, especially when the waters got deep or murky. I was never shy about asking Dolores for help when needed. She offered those words that day because I related events of the previous week that were particularly frustrating due to multiple power struggles with my three-year-old.

After listening to her advice, I said, "I know. Everyone says that. But honestly there are times when I'm so tired I feel like I could sleep until the middle of next year. I love my son more than anything in this world, but some days I just don't know how to cope with the challenges, not to mention the exhaustion." As I spoke those words I felt like anything but a candidate for "Mother of the Year."

"We have all been there, Honey. Most parents have thought their kids would be small forever and they'd never be able to keep up with the stresses that accompany the joys of childrearing. I always found it best in the tough times to remain calm, pray, and keep a sense of humor. The sweet, funny things are among the biggest blessings in parenting, and in life," she told me. "And most circumstances have a funny side you know."

I sighed and thanked her for the wise counsel. I was comforted by knowing at least I wasn't a bad parent who was losing control. I reasoned that perhaps I could try seeing life's events with a little more humor. I had no idea I would be called upon to put this new approach into practice a few weeks after our conversation.

One day my son, Gabe, was following me around with continuous chatter and requests. It seemed like every other minute he called, "Mom, Mom?"

His dad was out of town and his grandmother was visiting for the day. Although he loved his grandparents, it was his mother's attention he wanted that day.

It was a pleasant day filled with activities aimed at keeping a toddler busy. There were no power struggles or tantrums disrupting our time together. Still, about mid-afternoon, I began to feel weary. That's when Gabe's grandmother offered a suggestion. "Laura, why don't you go enjoy a hot bath and relax? Sometimes you just need to do something for you and not feel guilty about it. Explain to Gabe that you're going to be in the big bathroom for a little bit, but you are still close. He and I can take care of each other for that time."

I agreed, swept Gabe onto my lap and explained, "Gabriel, Mom is going to take a bath. When I get out of the tub, we'll help

Grammy make dinner. Then we'll all play later tonight. I'm going into the big bathroom now. I won't be far away. And I need you to do something for me."

He nodded his head with such enthusiasm I was encouraged to continue. "Now, for the time I'm in the bathroom, which is just going to be a little while, I need you to stay with Grammy. And you know how you like to call 'Mom' when you want me? Well, while I'm in there I don't want you calling 'Mom' okay?"

He smiled, nodded again, kissed my cheek, wiggled down from my lap, and went happily on his way with his favorite action figure. I smiled, feeling confident he took the instructions quite well. I was overjoyed, guilt-free, and already feeling renewed by the prospect of taking care of me.

I filled the bathtub with warm water and fragrant lavender bubbles. After pouring a steaming cup of herbal tea, I settled into what I thought would be a luscious half-hour without my little one requiring my attention. About ten minutes into my bliss I was marveling at how well my son was behaving. I knew Dolores had been right. A kind and clear explanation, while inwardly praying, was all that was needed.

Then I heard a knock on the bathroom door accompanied by Gabe's little voice. "Laura, Laura, you still in there?"

I took a deep breath, submerged into the bubbles. Blew out all the air and came up laughing. The little guy literally followed my exact instructions. I could almost hear Dolores giggling.

Just a few short months before I wrote this story, my handsome, thirty-two-year-old son took a bride. He walked into a journey that will include new adventures and challenges. I don't offer advice to him or his lovely wife other than to, on occasion, work in some words from my mentor and friend. "Keep a sense of humor. The sweet, funny things are among the biggest blessings in life. And almost all circumstances have a funny side."

Like most mothers I often reflect on the fact that, indeed, the years flew by without me being conscious of how fast time was moving. While my son was growing up, I treasured my few small patches of alone time. But today, in a season where my life has an abundance of alone time, I rejoice when I answer a ringing telephone and hear, "Mom?"

Reflection Question

Can you think of a time when an older friend or mentor offered advice, especially when you felt you were at the end of your rope? Did you remember to thank God for that advice and that person? If not, thank Him and them, if possible, now. Then be ready to offer mentoring or friendship to another in their time of need.

CHAPTER 9

Last Waltz

Trust in the LORD with all your heart and lean not on your own understanding.

—Proverbs 3:5

❧

FOR THE TALENTED, GENEROUS AND JOYFUL
GOLDEN, COLORADO ELVES

MY STOMACH RUMBLED IN response to the aroma of bacon and eggs served at tables covered with red and green cloths in a room bordered by decorated Christmas trees. I was grateful my gastric symphony was muffled by elated squeals from small children as Santa moved through the crowd taking gift requests. The annual Golden, Colorado, Santa's Breakfast was a huge success once again.

As the party wound down, singers invited the group to join in the last song. They offered a superb rendition of a Christmas ballad from the 1940s. Adults nodded in time to the music as they sang along. The tune encouraged listeners to be happy and put troubles behind them, at least for a season.

My troubles, however, were far from behind me. I delighted in attending these events in the past because I found them joyful and uplifting. For weeks before the occasion, I anticipated being surrounded by merriment and wonder expressed on faces of children, young and old. But holiday joy and I seemed to have parted company that year. I was struggling with an inner conflict fueled by recent internet chatter. Some people, including some close friends, believed secular celebrations diminished the sacredness of Christmas and prohibited God's real work from being done.

As a follower of Christ, I am thankful for the gift God gave to a broken world. My turmoil wasn't due to lack of belief in the "reason for the season." It was fed by the fact that I am an elf. To be precise, I am captain of the Golden, Colorado, Elves.

For several years I had gathered a group of other like-minded ladies willing to wear curl-toed shoes, pointy hats, elf ears, and red velvet costumes fringed in bells. I had always believed bringing pleasure to my community as I played this elf role was valuable, not detrimental. But after reading and hearing voices to the contrary, I began reassessing my role in stripping the sacred from the season.

I considered handing off my elf gear altogether because, in some way, I agreed with those voices online. There was, however, one factor that kept me on course. I had committed to the event organizers to be the one in charge of assembling the elves to accompany Santa on his merry journey. After a few sleepless nights, and a lot of prayer, I felt God calling me to keep that commitment. I chose to do elf duty just one more time.

That day, I was still feeling uneasy at perhaps doing the wrong thing by dishonoring God and my faith. I was so distracted that I almost missed the presence of a small child clinging to my right leg. I looked down and saw a sleepy-eyed little boy putting both arms in the air, signaling for me to lift him up. I surveyed the immediate area and saw a gray-haired woman, with a camera pointed in my direction, nodding her head at me. I assumed she was responsible for the small tyke and was granting me permission to honor his request.

As I held him, he looked me in the eyes, offered a shy smile, wrapped both arms around my neck and put his head on my shoulder. I began a slow waltz-like dance with him. He closed his eyes and within seconds dozed off. I thought he must have been no more than three years old because he felt weightless in my arms.

The singers harmonized to a tune reminding us of a simpler time when the warmth and value of the season meant just being with friends and loved ones. I was hypnotized by the serenade and closed my eyes too, moving in a small circle as I listened to the words. I didn't notice when the music ended and kept swaying until another elf tapped me on the shoulder. The child I held didn't stir until the lady with the camera came forward and took him from me. She handed him to another lady who began putting a coat on him.

The gray-haired woman took both my hands in hers and whispered, "Thank you. You made what I believe will be my little grandson's last Christmas special." I was silent, not knowing how to respond. "You see," she continued, "he's almost six years old and needs a new heart. The doctors haven't been successful in finding a suitable donor. They're telling us he can't make it more than a few months. We just continue praying and doing everything we can to make his limited time with us normal and joyful.

"You have helped us do that today. He's exhausted, as you can see. But it has been a long time since we've seen him smiling and at peace like this. Thank you again Miss Elf. God bless you." She kissed my cheek and headed out the door behind the woman carrying my sleepy little dance partner.

My words sounded muffled as they departed. "God bless you, my friend. I will pray for him too. I will pray for all of you."

The crowd moved around me in an effort to exit the room on their way to observe the Christmas parade. I remained immobile, as if my elf shoes were glued to the floor. But my heart pounded, and my mind moved like a jet gathering speed to take flight.

"Captain, are you okay? You look like you're about to cry. What's the trouble?" One of my lieutenant elves spoke, jolting me out of my private thoughts.

"No trouble at all. Go ahead to the parade staging area. Take the other elves with you, please. I'll be along soon. I just need a few minutes." My words sounded less than convincing, even to me.

I waited for the crowd to exit through the front door. Then I moved to a back exit that took me into an alley removed from the festive holiday scene. I leaned against the brick building and inhaled the crisp Colorado winter air heavy with a pending snowstorm. I made sure I was alone in the alley before I let a flood of tears break forth.

In part, my tears were from heartbreak over questions I knew would probably go unanswered. But there also were tears of gratitude because I hadn't given into the voices saying God couldn't use me to do His work within secular settings. I realized that by putting aside my need for human approval, God allowed me to bring a little boy, and his family, the love and peace Christmas is meant to impart. In that comical, clown-like costume representing earthly merriment God's work was brought to the human stage.

The last verse of the song played in my mind as I began collecting my emotions and moving toward my next destination. I heard words encouraging me to hang stars on my tree, enjoy the community of togetherness now, and hope we will be together again next Christmas.

I turned onto Main Street, picked my way through hundreds of people and soaked in the full beauty of the blessing. I understood God had given me the opportunity to hold a sick, and perhaps dying, child for a few moments and bring a little contentment into his young life.

My tears dried as I walked to the stage along with a large group of adults and children clamoring for pictures with an elf. I obliged as many as possible. Progress through the crowd was slow, but I wasn't in a hurry. I talked to people, shook hands, made eye contact, and wished the parade pilgrims a Merry Christmas.

I wondered about the child I held just moments before. Was he awake to watch this celebration? Would he see future celebrations if the doctors found a healthy heart to replace his ailing one? Or would he soon be in the midst of another parade with saints rejoicing as he entered the Kingdom and loving embrace of his Heavenly Father? My earlier grief gave some ground as I relaxed into understanding it was not necessary for me to have answers because I could trust the One who does.

As I stepped toward the bright lights and up the stage steps, I offered a silent prayer. "Thank you, God, for allowing me a small role in your work today. Thank you for the miraculous peace You gave that little one, his family and me."

The parade began. The elves danced and entertained people along the streets of downtown Golden. With every handshake, bright smile, or wish for a blessed season, I felt more certain God's joy danced with and through us, even in a secular celebratory setting.

Reflection Notes

There is a fine line between the secular and the sacred in a variety of situations. Although we are called to be salt and light to the world, does that mean we reject anything we cannot categorize as sacred? Is the sacred work of the Holy Spirit only done in assigned areas of what we see as church or Christ-related settings? Notice today where God may be calling you to do His work in the earthly realm.

CHAPTER 10

The Right Road

"The Bible teaches us that we are blessed not just so that we can feel good, not just so we can be happy and comfortable, but so that we will bless others."

—Rick Warren

჻

FOR PEOPLE I OFTEN OVERLOOK IN MY HASTE
TO SERVE THEM

"THIS IS WHY I hate taking this street!" I complained to myself as I gripped the steering wheel while sitting in a traffic jam on an errand to deliver scarves made by my knitting

group. I was on my way to an organization
that would distribute them to homeless
shelters. I volunteered to take them because
the receiving center was near my home. They
were open for only a few more minutes, and I
was running out of time. My usual route was
blocked because of road construction, and I
was forced to take another street. My choice,
it appeared, was a mistake due to congested
traffic. My car's thermometer registered the
outside temperature at ten degrees. It began
snowing, and the wind picked up diminishing
my visibility. I grew more annoyed with each
new complication, which made the drive more
difficult.

Obviously, grumbling wasn't doing anything
but fueling more frustration, so I decided to
occupy my mind with something constructive.
I tried figuring out what to do with the scarves
in the trunk of my car if I couldn't make it to
the center in the next several minutes. While

pondering my options, I noticed a man pushing a woman in a wheelchair toward a corner bus stop. She was bent forward with her head close to her lap, protecting her face from the cold wind. She had a blanket pulled around her shoulders.

Guilt flooded me as I realized I was complaining about a minor inconvenience compared to others who were in far worse shape than me. A small voice in my head hinted, "It looks like she could use a warm scarf."

The car behind me honked, alerting me that vehicles were moving forward. Instead of going straight as planned, I turned right and pulled into the parking lot adjacent to the bus stop. I jumped from my car, opened the trunk, and grabbed the first scarf I saw. It was made of heavy aqua wool. As I was admiring the workmanship, I noticed lights from an approaching bus were visible in the distance through heavy snow. I knew if I was going to reach the scarf's recipient, I had to run.

When I approached the couple, I was out of breath. They weren't that far away, but the cold air forced me to take short, shallow breaths. The woman looked up as I held out the scarf. Her eyes widened, but she didn't move. I stepped closer and wrapped the scarf around her neck, tucking it under the blanket.

Between quick breaths I said, "This is for you. I think it goes with your eyes. What do you think?"

She nodded and opened her blanket. "It matches my sweatshirt too. How did you know?"

Tears filled her eyes. "Thank you, dear. Look, it's perfect."

I bent over and kissed her on the forehead but had no time to say more. The bus pulled up to the curb and lowered its ramp to accommodate the wheelchair. I stood back and watched her companion and the bus driver maneuver her chair up the ramp. She turned and blew a kiss to me from her window seat as the bus pulled away. I waved and walked back to my car.

According to my watch, it was past closing time at the distribution center. I re-entered the line of clogged traffic and relaxed in the warmth of my car. The journey's end, and the time it took to get there, didn't seem so important. There would be homes for all of the scarves, as there was for this one. I just needed to slow down long enough to see the needs around me instead of setting an agenda for how, and where, they were to be given.

My car thermometer showed the temperatures plummeting, but I felt warmth from the memory of a smile and blown kiss of gratitude for a gift given to a stranger. I said a prayer for the lady in the aqua sweatshirt (and

now matching scarf), as well as her companion.
Then, along with many other motorists, I began
the slow progression on a road that was not my
first choice, but definitely was the right one.

Reflection Notes

We live in busyness and schedules dictated by "to-
do" lists. Some days it feels like we rush from one
thing to the other. Even if we are trying to do God's
will, do we hand the outcome to Him and then trust
Him to bring about the means of accomplishing that?
How might life look different if we intentionally
yielded our own intentions?

CHAPTER 11

Masked

"The worst loneliness is to not be comfortable with yourself."

—Mark Twain

FOR ME

I PERFORMED THE DANCE in a mime costume complete with a white, expressionless mask covering my face. Audience members depended on my movements to tell the story. The music had words, but I chose to portray someone who felt safer expressing those words behind a mask.

77

At the conclusion of the piece I hurried backstage, removed the mask, ran my fingers through my hair, and sighed, "Ahh, now that's better. It's tough working behind a mask." Other troupe members nodded in agreement.

Wearing a mask is difficult for many reasons. Peripheral vision is diminished. Obstructed vision limits perception of personal space. That limitation can impair balance and cause the wearer to proceed with caution in an attempt to avoid injury. It takes a lot of energy to compensate for these conditions, which can lead to exhaustion in little time. Despite the drawbacks, however, a mask can provide something that many (like the little mime) crave: safety.

In the months since that performance, I've become aware of how many times I subject myself to the tiresome endeavor of being in disguise. Often I do not present my authentic self for fear of rejection or disapproval. This may be due to lessons I learned as a child, or memories ingrained as I danced with life's disagreeable experiences over the past six decades.

Being in disguise can be a challenge. Your vision is restricted, compromising your balance and making it difficult to navigate obstacles, perceived or real. I sometimes don't realize the energy I'm expending while trying to avoid injury. Many days it's just plain easier to don the mask, be what others expect, and move with calculated caution through life. Those are the days when I realize that I've strayed from God and His will for my life.

These times are less frequent as I grow older because I've learned that the closer I walk with the Lord, the more I find deep peace in the truth that He accepts me just as I am. I've learned that any mask I attempt to wear is invisible to Him anyway. This sustains me when I'm unable to extricate myself from situations where I feel the need to be silent and safe, regardless of the cost.

I prefer to never feel restricted or unbalanced. I try not to volunteer to be in circumstances that will deplete my energy. When I do find myself in those situations, however, I can rely on the knowledge that I have a place to turn for rest and acceptance. I can remember the One who always welcomes me with love, beyond pretenses. This, I think, is part of the peace He promises that passes all human understanding. I look forward to, and am grateful for, the times when I sit down with my Heavenly Father, sigh in relief, remove the masks of the day, and say, "Ah, now that's better."

Reflection Notes

As you walk your day, your week, your life, try to be aware of when you feel uncomfortable enough to rely on pretenses that may or may not help you feel accepted in certain circles. Ask God to keep His truth before you—you are beloved, lovable, and worthy of love—just as you are.

CHAPTER 12

One Foot
and Then the Other

"To what will you look for help if you will not look to that which is stronger than yourself?"
—C. S. Lewis, *Mere Christianity*

FOR EVERYONE WHO HAS HAD TO MAKE THE AGONIZING DECISION OF ORGAN DONATION AFTER DEATH OF A LOVED ONE

IT IS VERY QUIET in the donor room. I try not to imagine the sounds made only days ago by the six-year-old boy now lying motionless, lifeless, under the paper drapes that cover the sterile surgical field. Instead I move through the setup of instruments, sponges, and sutures.

It is hard to resist temptation to wonder if he played baseball, had a sister whose hair he pulled, or squealed with glee as he wrestled his dog. I push away the image of him fighting bedtime before saying goodnight to his mother. "I love you, Mommy."

I call all my training to the front lines in the battle to silence my heart. I focus on the rhythmic hum of the breathing machine pushing oxygen to organs we will harvest and place in other children's ailing bodies. Despite my intense focus on the precious little gentleman in our care, the machine's voice stays on the periphery of the oppressive silence resting in the room.

The surgeon stretches his hand toward me. For a little more than a second, we make eye contact. He says nothing. I need no words. I place the scalpel in his hand, and it begins.

At twenty-six years old, I am a skilled and practiced surgical technician. I know this is not the time to attempt dialogue. I don't expect the banter and camaraderie I've come to enjoy in other operating rooms and different situations. Gurneys carrying patients roll past the closed door but are of no consequence to me. I take no notice of chatter at the scrub sinks.

I don't dare step from behind my mask of honed skills to ask the question that will reveal my humanity. I stay well-guarded in the busyness of routine. I move methodically, efficiently, thinking carefully about my task— the mental equivalent of putting one foot forward and then the other. I proceed alongside the doctor who is also stepping forward with one foot and then the other. We have done this dance before. We know the choreography by heart.

This child is my patient. He has been declared dead by medical and legal criteria. But in this room, in this hour, under these lights, and with all I have, I offer the gentlest of care for his dignity. Touching his leg that's draped with a sterile sheet, I attempt to connect with his young soul and let him know someone is here. He is not alone in these last, silent hours.

The surgeon puts his hand out. I respond. I place one metaphorical foot in front of the other. My eyes are the only visible part of my face. I will them to continue scanning the field in anticipation of the physician's needs and order them to lock tears behind stoic lenses unclouded by cataracts of emotion while, with tenderness, I hold in gloved hands the sacred hush. I am one of the last to feel life's warmth in this little frame. I am noiseless as I again touch the small draped leg close to where I stand.

At the procedure's conclusion, I attend to legalities, filling out paperwork. I head to the locker room, strip off my surgical clothes, and step into the shower. With hot, pulsing water cascading over me, I wait for the answer that my youthful mind insists will come if I just keep asking. I rest in the void of the unanswered query. Weak and tired, I surrender.

There are people I work with who say we cannot always know reasons for some earthly experiences. Still, my coworkers believe a power greater than us has the answers. Tonight, like never before, my heart craves their faith, their wisdom, their understanding. I find comfort in the words they've spoken. And I allow those words to flow over me with the tumbling water and unanswered question.

When I step from the shower, I dress and leave before the rest of the OR crew gathers for our weekly pilgrimage to the College Inn for enchiladas and half-priced drafts. No food or drink tonight. Not tonight. I start the short walk to my apartment on the edge of the hospital campus. I am alone.

My shoulders slump with heaviness as I think, not for the first time, about the boy's parents. Where are they? Do they know their treasured child was not alone in the end? Do they understand he was treated with tenderness and love even as we disconnected the breathing machines? Are they holding each other in the shadows of both losing and giving hope with the stroke of a pen?

I'm two blocks from the hospital. It is safe to cry now. No permission is needed; none is sought. I move on and am careful to place one foot and then the other. My thoughts return to the words of faith shared by coworkers. I sense a presence I do not know but welcome into my silent space.

Now it is okay to ask, "Why?" Only this one word accompanies me on my journey.

Tomorrow I will start a new day and return to work. Perhaps I will help alleviate suffering by assisting with a gallbladder removal or repair of a broken hip. Maybe I will witness the miracle of new life at a baby's birth. But tonight, tonight I think only of the little boy who slipped from this world into the next with me at his side.

At home I sit bathed in dim light. I am motionless, pensive, in awe of life, with respect for death. And I remain very quiet.

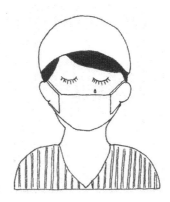

Reflection Notes

Can you recall a time when no matter how much you sought an answer, there just was not one to be found? Can you look back now and see that even in your deepest times of suffering, Jesus was there? If suffering is part of the human condition, is it possible we can know our Lord more intimately within the walls of our pain and confusion?

CHAPTER 13

Impossible

"If we have no peace, it is because we have forgotten we belong to each other."
—Mother Teresa

❧

FOR GABRIEL, SAMANTHA,
ORIN, AND LISA

"HOW CAN THIS BE possible?" I ask my two tablemates.

"How can what be possible?" replies one of my companions.

"You two sitting here, drinking tea and chatting like lifelong friends. It just isn't possible and should not be happening. That's all there is to it."

"Why?"

I take a deep breath and try explaining what, to me, is obvious. "Because you are a . . . well, you're a dog, and she's a rabbit."

"Yes, she is a rabbit and I am a dog. That's true." Dog empties his cup; then offers it to Rabbit who fills it again.

"By all that is natural and normal, you are enemies." I speak using my most authoritative voice.

"Are we?" the dog asks.

I'm trying to decide if this dog is teasing me. At the same time, I wonder about the rabbit. I can't understand why she is so calm. He could devour her in one chomp. "Yes. In the animal kingdom dogs chase and eat rabbits while rabbits run and hide from dogs."

"How do you know that?" Rabbit asks, speaking for the first time. Her voice is not as soft as I expect. I'm surprised by the tranquil strength she exudes as she pours tea.

"I know because I have been taught that. Everyone knows that. It's in books."

"What are books?" Dog asks, leaning on the table with his forelegs pointed in my direction.

"What are books!?" I gasp. "Never mind that now. This rabbit should be running for all she's worth, if she wants to stay alive." Despite attempts to the contrary, my impatience laces every word.

"Should she?" Dog asks. The corners of his mouth turn upward in an almost undetectable smile that makes me think he's just having a game with me. I know at any moment he's going to put his enormous mouth on her tiny head and have a snack.

"What about you?" I ask Rabbit, imploring her to enter this conversation. "What do you have to say?"

Rabbit pauses and takes a deep breath. "I say it's time for another pot of tea." She raises one paw to attract the server's attention.

"No, no, no. This isn't about tea."

Rabbit looks at Dog and then back to me. "Would you rather have coffee?"

My bottom jaw drops to my breastbone and silence tumbles into my teacup. Dog sits back in his chair and eyes me. I begin to wonder if I'm the snack this morning.

I shake my head and return to my original question. "How can this be possible?"

Dog follows suit by repeating one of *his* original queries. "Why . . ." he begins while watching Rabbit as she pours more tea. "She has nothing to fear from me. She is my friend."

"Look, Mr. Dog. I mean no disrespect, but you eat meat, right? She is meat."

"Yes. Do you eat meat?" Dog issues a full smile now in what I believe is canine humor meant to mock a less-wise human.

"Yes but . . ."

"Do you eat your friends?"

"Don't be ridiculous; of course not. And you are changing the subject. You have nothing in common. You are enemies, plain and simple. You always have been and always will be."

"I see." Dog scratches his chin with one paw.

"We both like tea." The sound of Rabbit's voice startles me. I've almost forgotten she's at the table. I jump, spilling hot tea on my right index finger.

"Ouch." I put my finger in my mouth and sit in confused suspicion as I look from one to the other.

Dog uses his large, hairy paw to bring my wounded digit back to the table. He leans down and licks my new wound. His gentle touch dismisses my fear of being on his menu.

"We have many things in common even though we have many differences." He looks around us. I follow his gaze. We are sitting at a small table outside a coffeehouse in the mountains of Colorado. We're beside a clear stream carrying melted snow from high peaks that will provide water to the flatter lands. The waves in the water are various sizes. They flow at rapid speed, separate yet together, moving toward the same destination. They've no time to question solidarity.

My attention is drawn to three birds of different colors and sizes perched on a nearby tree branch. They perform a composition in three-part harmony that sends shivers of pleasure through my small frame. Dog nods as if he hears percussion in the little concert. I marvel at him and Rabbit in their unhurried, peaceful, shared relaxation.

Rabbit puts her delicate paw under my chin and lifts my head skyward. I gaze through green leaves and see an array of blue hues on an infinite canvas. The three of us follow movement of clouds chasing each other on their celestial journey. As we gaze upward together, I am brought into a secret corridor of their understanding. I become relaxed, at peace, content.

"I see," I mutter. They are the only words I have uttered in several minutes.

Rabbit breaks the trance when announcing she must attend to her young. She departs under the brush and long grasses bordering the stream. Dog clears his throat.

"My humans will be concerned. It's my lunchtime. I never miss lunchtime. You know us dogs must have our meat." He winks and takes his leave.

~ ~ ~

My smile unmasks my joy of discovery, and I break into laughter. A voice interrupts my musings. "Honey, are you okay?" The voice belongs to my husband.

"Honey, wake up. Who are you talking to? Why are you laughing?"

As he nudges me awake, my eyes focus, and I attempt to explain. "Keith I've had the most extraordinary experience. There was a rabbit and a dog and tea and . . ."

"I know, Love. But it was only a dream. Tell me in the morning. It'll be dawn soon." He kisses my forehead and rolls over onto his side.

"No, no Keith. It was real." My protests are lost as slumber recaptures him.

The clock says it's a few hours past midnight, but for me it is already a new dawning. I get out of bed and move to the living room. Out of habit I reach for the remote control and turn on the TV.

A world leader is speaking to a cheering crowd of people. Those present raise their voices in enthusiastic roars of approval.

"We must never forget those different from us are our enemies. We don't have beliefs, habits, or cultures in common. They'll present a real threat if we allow them to bring their lifestyles into our country. I am telling you they will eat us for dinner if we don't prevent it. It is them or us."

Cheers and applause rise to an ear-splitting level.

"We must never forget they have always been our enemies. History tells us that. It's been recorded in books throughout centuries. They will always be our adversaries. We'll never see eye to eye or have common values. Why I bet they even eat different food than us."

The crowd erupts in laughter and pumps their fists in the air. He joins them in both.

I turn off the TV, hug my legs into my chest, and rest my forehead on my knees. Keith's right; it was only a dream. It just seemed so real to me. A tear comes to my eye and does its best to defy gravity but loses. I try to slow its progress by wiping it with my right index finger. The salty liquid stings and I pull my hand away. In the moonlight, coming from an open window, I stare at a little raised blister on my wounded right paw.

Reflection Notes

Do you believe in visions? I've had some visions that I've paid attention to and some I've ignored. Here is one I am glad I embraced. It started as I walked by the Blue River in Silverthorne, Colorado. There I saw a sculpture of a dog and rabbit sitting at a table, having tea and a chat. I sat down by the river and God gave me a vision of what peace between diverse populations could look like. Have you ever wondered how that may look? Take a moment and ask God to show you His vision of unity. Then ask what your part might be in that reality—in your neighborhood, church, community, or the world.

CHAPTER 14

Waiting on the Pilot

Those who are kind benefit themselves, but the cruel bring ruin on themselves.
—Proverbs 11:17

FOR TRAVELERS

THROUGH MANY YEARS OF travel, I have learned it's vital to avoid two things while moving through airports. Do not argue with TSA agents and do not engage in conflicts with other passengers. I have no trouble keeping my mouth shut when going through security screens. However, controlling my tongue when another passenger becomes obnoxious is sometimes a challenge.

As I grow older, I tend to tolerate more bad behavior than I used to. That does not, however, include bullying of any kind. I can be less than shy about making my feelings known. So I never travel without my husband of over twenty-five years. My spouse has been known to lean into me slightly and give a little nudge in an effort to help me think before speaking. He only does this when he feels I need to employ a filter that may save an unpleasant verbal altercation. However, if we become separated, I can land in a struggle between common sense and my desire to right all that's wrong (in my opinion) with the world.

One such struggle occurred during a recent trip from Milwaukee to Denver. My husband boarded the plane before I did, and I was left to witness the antics of a disagreeable passenger. Once again I was reminded that God is always flying alongside me, even when I feel stranded.

Between my husband's boarding group and mine, families with small children were called to board. Among this group was a young woman with two toddlers and an infant. The baby was crying and struggling in her mother's arms.

The attendant scanning boarding passes stopped and looked at the young mother. "The computer is not allowing me to scan the bar code on your pass, ma'am. I'm sorry, but I can't allow you on the plane."

The young mother said she bought the tickets weeks ago and printed her passes off that morning. She shifted the baby from one hip to the other, reached in her bag and produced an ID for the attendant to inspect.

After checking the ID and referring to her computer screen, the attendant said, "You are scheduled for this flight, but the bar code is being rejected. If you didn't have the pass, you couldn't have gotten past security. I'll have to look into this." As the attendant stepped from her post and moved to another computer terminal she informed the waiting passengers, "We'll have a slight delay, folks."

"Great, that's all we need, clueless people creating problems for everyone," bellowed a woman to my left who spoke at a volume, I suspected, to ensure her insult was heard by all in the terminal. "What's wrong with people that they can't figure out how to do things right?" She continued to berate as she scowled at the mother and her children.

Another attendant tried to infuse calm into the situation. "Ma'am, there has been a mistake. These people are scheduled to be on this plane, but there's a computer glitch. It's not anyone's fault. We're checking into it and will get going as soon as possible."

"That's not good enough. I've had to postpone a business meeting due to delays caused by this rotten weather. Now, thanks to incompetence all around, I may miss that meeting altogether." The inconvenienced passenger spoke while never removing her eyes from the woman holding her infant and doing her best to keep two rambunctious tiny tots under control.

The complainer was getting louder, and my temper was rising. I assessed my options. I could keep quiet or tell her to get a grip and risk an altercation that might render me an overnight guest of the city of Milwaukee. I prayed, "Lord, you know me. You know I hate bullies. Please, please help this little family. Mostly, please help me keep my mouth shut since my filter is on the plane."

Just then a small, gray-haired woman to my right leaned into me and with almost undetectable contact gave me a slight nudge.

When I looked at her, she shook her head from side to side. I know nothing is beyond the capabilities of God. But in my book, this ranked right up there with His parting of the Red Sea. Somehow the Lord had either channeled my hubby through this little lady by mental telepathy, or my spouse was both in the plane and the boarding line—in disguise—at the same time.

I accepted the stranger's support and nodded my head as I whistled to myself in amazement at the God who responded without delay to my distress call. The gray-haired angel's lips turned up in a little smile.

The attendant brought an update. "There has been a glitch in the system, and some ticketed passengers are not registered in the computer. We'll resume boarding in a few minutes."

"I will never fly this airline again," announced the businesswoman. "This is absurd. Just leave them here and let's go. Some of us have lives. We can't be held up by a bunch of people who have no idea how to travel and don't care if they inconvenience everyone."

For a second, I took my eyes off the gray-haired woman on my right and turned my blazing Irish-Italian eyes to the obnoxious woman on my left. Then I heard God say, "Leave it."

I turned my gaze to the young mother who was flush and looked as if she was about to cry. She eyed the shouting woman, then looked at the rest of us in line. My new friend leaned in closer, and I bit my tongue. I offered what I hoped was a reassuring nod and smile to the young lady and her children. In silence, I prayed for temper control.

Within five minutes, we resumed boarding. The protester, who was originally behind me in line, pushed ahead of me and slammed her boarding pass down on the podium for the attendant's inspection. I took a long, deep breath and continued petitioning the Holy One for a temporary case of lockjaw.

The attendant looked up. "Oh, I'm sorry, ma'am. You're at the wrong gate. You were supposed to board three gates down from here. I'm afraid your plane took off ten minutes ago."

I sucked my smile onto the back of my front teeth and directed my gaze to my forty-dollar brand-name sneaker knock-offs. I didn't dare look in the direction of the angry traveler. I knew I would give away my delight at this outcome. I asked God to forgive me for finding joy in another's misfortune. I also thanked Him for the special filter He sent in the form of a sweet stranger.

The attendant reached beyond her and asked for my pass. As I walked the ramp, I felt a hand on my right elbow. My new friend, and extra conscience, patted my arm. I thanked her, and I thanked God again for patting my arm in line with the assurance that I didn't need to intervene in the conflict.

After all ticketed passengers bordered the plane, including the little family with the rejected bar codes, we headed for Denver. When we were airborne, my husband asked what postponed the boarding. I smiled and explained, "We were just waiting on the Pilot."

Reflection Notes

Where do you struggle to resist taking control of situations when in fact your interference may make no difference or may even make things worse? Can you think of one of those times? If you turned to God for help, how did He resolve the issue(s)?

CHAPTER 15

The Mortar Man Cometh

Is not wisdom found among the aged? Does not long life bring understanding?
—Job 12:12, NET

❧

FOR BETTY AND DOLORES

DESPITE MODERN-DAY MESSAGES TO the contrary, the aging process can represent a glorious time filled with gifts not necessarily available in our youth. One of those is wisdom we gain that affords us critical thinking skills. These are especially useful when making healthy choices for our well-being. For example, we can choose to fight to retain our youth, which is impossible in reality. Or we can elect to accept ourselves, even with signs of aging, as we grow older. I'm not saying we shouldn't try to look and feel our best, but we should understand the futility of buying into the culture's definitions of what our best should be. Basically, it all depends on whether we choose to listen to the world's view of aging or to God's view.

This point was brought home to me one morning as I walked in a mall, after an exercise class, and sipped on a hot vanilla latte. A salesman emerged from behind a kiosk with a pitch aimed at convincing me I couldn't possibly pass up the opportunity to purchase his age-reversing face cream.

He made an attempt (unsolicited) to guess my age. He tried flattering me by offering an estimate that was twenty years younger than my actual age. He then told me what he did not like about my face. In his opinion, my wrinkles had to go. It was fortunate for me that he had just the product to fill in the cracks, smooth out my face, and make it "real pretty."

This is where my mind checked out and I politely nodded like a bobble headed dog in the back of a 1960 Cadillac. I wasn't trying to be discourteous, but my thoughts wandered to the image of a former neighbor. When I was a little girl, we lived next door to a man named Mr. Mueller. Every day he went to work in his big white panel truck, dressed in overalls and a checkered shirt. He carried a metal slate with a handle and a small tool with a triangular blade called a trowel. He was a bricklayer, and these were the tools of his trade.

One day I asked Mr. Mueller about these interesting gadgets. He informed me that he used them to mix up something called mortar and put it into cracks between bricks. The mortar, he told me, held the bricks in place, filled in the cracks, and made brickwork look real pretty and smooth.

I heard someone cough, realized I was being rude with my mental time travel, and came back into the company of this modern-day mortar man who didn't like my face. He offered to do his magic by smoothing the rough parts of my face and making me look more desirable. His smile faded as I looked past him in anticipation of seeing my childhood neighbor. The anti-aging guru stepped around me to try his luck with the next potential customer. I moved on and enjoyed my latte.

That night, I couldn't help studying my mug in the mirror. I made faces trying to find what needed to be plastered up. I smiled and then frowned. I wanted to see why I simply could not live without a half-ounce jar of a concoction developed to make my face acceptable.

As I began my survey, I was struck by the stories reflecting back at me. I saw a little girl who survived a family riddled with alcoholism, domestic violence, and abuse. Some smile wrinkles represent the madness of my early twenties with the parties, music, protests, and fierce intensity spent on self-definition. Other lines fade into strokes of sadness as I thought about many friends who never returned from Vietnam. Still other lines represent fury at the injustice my sisters and brothers of color have experienced, and still are experiencing, at being denied something that is supposed to be guaranteed in our country—equitable treatment on all levels.

I ran a forefinger over creases signifying indescribable joy when I first held my child after his birth. These lines sit next to those carved from anguish felt when standing beside others as they buried their precious babies.

Tears filled my eyes when I remembered the night I found and accepted Jesus. I rocked gently in the rhythm of the dance we've done for over forty years. In gratitude to Him, I acknowledged the blessings of family, friends, and the opportunity to grow through forgiving and being forgiven.

In my face that night, I saw tracks of a lifetime that has seen good and bad, joy and disappointment, fear and faith, love and loss, and the precious gift of over six decades on this earth. Although I have never considered myself a traffic-stopping beauty, I was puzzled to think my face could be considered offensive to someone with no understanding of the treasure represented by each fold or furrow. I sent up a little prayer asking God to protect that young man and many others in our society from being brainwashed by the sales pitch he had memorized.

I turned off the light and headed to bed. While submerging into a pillow, our Lord played a musical poem and guided me into dreams. Even in semi-consciousness, I knew God was revealing His truth about beauty and who defines it.

"I've put you dear one in this time and this space
Sculpted your life, plotted the course of your race
And even though life is both leather and lace
There is nothing, sweet child
I don't love on your face."

Reflection Notes

In an age and culture that says beauty is defined by the years on a calendar, how do you find your attitude about aging? Are you able to look into the mirror and see the beauty God sees in you no matter what your age or stage? Are you able to look at another man or woman and see their years as assets to be respected instead of a road map to be feared? Ask God today to help you immunize against a world that says your worth is defined by what others see as valuable and beautiful.

CHAPTER 16

I Am Here

Cast all your anxiety on him because he cares for you.
—1 Peter 5:7

FOR KEITH, A MAN WHO RESTS IN GOD

"I AM HERE LORD," I said through a yawn as I sat wrapped in a woolen blanket, clutching a cup of hot tea while sitting on the second-story deck of our mountain condo.

I had awakened a few minutes before 5 a.m. on a mid-September morning and envied my husband's ability to sleep. He was determined to get every bit of rest out of this vacation in Silverthorne, Colorado. I managed to find my robe and slippers, leave the bedroom in silence, make a cup of tea, drag a blanket behind me, and go out onto the deck to await the sunrise.

I knew it was God calling me to this space before the day's activity began. In my stupor-like mind-set, I tried to obey. Cool mountain air tempted me to dismiss the inviting voice in my head as an auditory hallucination and return to the warmth of my bed. Instead, I stared at the starless sky and waited for dawn's appearance. There are few places I feel as awed by God, the finest of artists, as I do in the mountains of my home state just before morning's early light. Like an expectant audience member, I awaited another of His spectacular creations. The black tea kicked my senses into gear as I listened to the morning blue jays' wake-up call.

"I am here, Lord." I repeated the announcement in case He missed it the first time around.

I waited. After several minutes the birds fell silent. In the stillness, as the caffeine infused my sleepy brain cells, I returned to concerns of recent weeks. There were problems to think about and worries to resume. I asked God, not for the first time, to reveal His plans for decisions I needed to make. I confessed my confusion and fear, again, as I had many times in our quiet times together. "I am here, Lord."

The light in the eastern sky grew in hues of gray, pink, mauve, and orange. The shapes of trees emerged. After waiting a few more minutes, I decided that I had gotten my spiritual signals crossed and could do my worrying inside where the temperature was more inviting. As I stood and began gathering my empty tea cup and blanket, I heard something. At first it was almost inaudible. I stayed motionless and listened. There was the sound—a slight whisper of air. It was not a wind exactly, but definitely it was more than a breeze. The aspen trees, now beginning their morning bath in the warming sunshine, stood still. I sensed a lulling, rhythmic presence. I felt it, even if the trees didn't.

I returned to my seat and again called, "I am here, Lord."

In the morning that was silent, other than the barely discernible air movement, I heard what I had been waiting to hear: "So am I, beloved daughter. Let's talk."

Reflection Notes

Jesus sought time alone with God on multiple occasions. He sat and waited patiently for His Father to give Him an audience, comfort, and encouragement. Modern-day contemplative souls, as well as spiritual leaders from many generations ago, encourage us to find time to wait and listen for the voice of God, away from the crowds and busyness of our world. If you haven't started a practice like this, perhaps it is time to ask God if He can show you how to enter into silence, and focus, during time carved out just for listening to Him.

CHAPTER 17

Finding Joy
in the Pouring Pain

*Nehemiah said, "Go and enjoy choice food and
sweet drinks, and send some to those who have
nothing prepared. This day is holy to our Lord.
Do not grieve, for the joy of the LORD is your
strength."*

—Nehemiah 8:10

FOR THOSE IN THE THROES OF DESPAIR

WAS MY FRIEND OUT of her mind? How
could she say we can have joy no matter what
our circumstances? Wasn't I sitting in this chair

a few weeks after a car accident that left me with two swollen, bruised knees and five displaced ribs? The physical pain paled in comparison to the guilt load that reminded me the wreck was undeniably my fault. I totaled two cars and hurt another driver. If my knees could have bent, I would have kicked my rear end.

Didn't I just receive news of a devastating tragedy that befell a family I adored? Hadn't I been made aware, again, of a relationship that no matter what I do may never be healed or restored? How do you find joy in the face of stories about one family member being mistreated at the hands of another?

But there my friend sat as we had coffee one day saying it really is possible to have joy no matter what trials we're facing. I love my friend. I usually left our meetings comforted with nuggets of truth and wisdom. That was not the case that day because, despite her words, I chose to rage against the stubborn silence standing like a granite wall in front of my questions.

How could I have been so careless as to cause an awful accident? Why did my friend's family have to suffer heart-stopping loss at the death of a child? How was I able to see myself as a Christian when I had a person in my life who found reason to hate me and slammed the door on my attempts at reconciliation? How could I minister to one hurt family member and still forgive the one who abused her?

I spent the next several mornings on my back porch meditating and watching rain fall. It seemed it was going to rain forever. Worse, yet, it seemed like it *had* been raining forever. And like the continuous rain, more questions dropped into my thoughts only to be met with more unnerving quiet.

One particularly wet, bleak morning, I stared full into the faces of my triple enemies: anger, guilt, and confusion. I couldn't believe all this happened within a month. I fought, I reasoned, and I demanded answers. All that came was the flood of water from menacing clouds that mirrored my dark despair.

Verbal sparring with God was not working. I threw my pain-racked body onto a couch and beat my fists into pillows as if I could extract a truth that would take away grief, guilt, and helplessness.

My ribs groaned, and my knees sent sharp, protesting throbs all the way to my toes. Finally, out of physical and mental exhaustion, I plummeted into a place I feared would be my emotional home for months. I made a conscious decision to surrender, lay down the tools of battle, and let go. It continued to rain. I continued to pour my heart out to God.

Then I heard it. It was faint at first but grew louder as my sobs subsided. The sound of children playing in our neighbor's backyard lifted to my ears like a song. I pulled my tear-soaked, limping self to the patio door and opened it to hear them better.

How could the little ones be playing, laughing, and even squabbling on this gloomy day? Didn't they know many worlds had been rocked by indescribable sadness? Didn't they know my heart was breaking for all that was broken in my world, the worlds of several people I loved, and one I never met before I demolished her car and sent her to the hospital? Didn't they know it was cold and rainy outside?

No, they knew nothing of the events or weather. All they knew was they were going to live and laugh today, no matter what nature or the world presented. In their pure childish wisdom, they rejected the troubles of the day and the external elements.

I stepped outside, stood in the rain, and listened to their squeals as I looked over the hedge separating our yards. They jumped in puddles and delighted in this, even this, frigid downpour. They danced in pools among patches of green grass nurtured by the relentless moisture.

The jubilant chorus of song and dance caught the attention of a few robins flitting from tree to tree. The birds added their voices to the symphony. I breathed in the smell of clean air and thanked God for laughing children, singing robins, and refreshing rain.

I moved closer to the hedge as water dripped off my hair and onto my face. "Hi, Miss Laura," they called in unison between giggles. I blew a kiss to the youngsters.

The guilt returned to the foreground of my thoughts. How could I allow myself to be pulled into their blissful world? I shouldn't feel joy on any level. It wasn't time.

But I did feel momentary elation. For a brief moment my heart lifted as I saw mental clouds, if not celestial ones, parting. I remembered a quote I heard about joy being a spiritual discipline requiring practice, patience, and persistence. New questions surfaced. How does one get their joy back when it has gone? What does it mean to be disciplined? Was my heart so heavy because I am undisciplined, unintelligent, or unable to make sense of a world that can often be senseless?

"You want some lunch, Honey? Please come in now. It's cold, and you're not dressed for this weather today." My husband's voice interrupted my queries.

"In a minute," I answered. I couldn't leave the moment. There were still unanswered questions. I thought maybe, just maybe, answers were in the sights, sounds, and smells of this early May scene playing out before and around me. I opened my right hand, allowing the rain to hit my palm. I stared at each drop and prayed that one held the key that would unlock the door to my self-imposed pain prison.

When I went inside, I ate without conversing. I would not change clothes even though I was wet and cold. My husband didn't attempt to derail me from the journey I chose.

After lunch, I went to my prayer room to be alone with God. As I started my little water fountain and lit a candle, I reflected on what I remembered earlier. "Joy is a spiritual discipline. Like all disciplines it takes practice, patience, and persistence to find and keep."

I blew out the match and dropped my head. "Okay, Lord."

As I once again wept the tears of surrender, God began to reveal a meaning of spiritual discipline. I discovered that discipline is found in intentional seeking. It is in the awareness of children's voices, new spring growth, tiny birds, and cleansing heavenly waters that minister to a hurting soul. It is in not allowing guilt to overshadow the delights of the day I'm given to live. It is in knowing that no matter how heavy our pain, Jesus is there to help bear the load and hold us up if we choose to partner with Him on the road to restoration. I saw all of God's gentle offerings that day as confirmation of His healing presence. I understood that a journey toward wholeness was available.

The hard work of spiritual discipline is found in an obedient posture of seeking but not demanding answers. No matter what the question, joy is about resting in the One who has the answers, and still trusting Him when the answers are slow in coming or are never revealed at all.

I resolved to no longer dishonor myself by shoving my grief under a pillow of anger. Instead I chose to give myself the space needed to process that which may not ever be processed thoroughly. I opened up to healing. And I committed to practice, patience, and persistence until I found the laughter, singing birds, and love that are all around.

When I turned off the fountain, blew out the candle, and returned to my long to-do list, I held a new belief. Eventually the joyful moments would stay longer and crowd out, or minimize, the moments of hopelessness and helplessness. My anger and fighting were ways to prematurely close the gap from pain to resolution, without learning what precious lessons are in the chasm.

I moved slowly (very slowly) out of my special space, found my husband, took his hand, and kissed his forehead. For a bit of time we sat on the back porch just watching it rain. He broke the silence first by asking if I was feeling better.

I said, "Maybe just a little. But I now know I can survive in the hard places while waiting for the day when I am restored."

I leaned my head against Keith's reassuring shoulder and thanked God for a kind, patient husband. Before drifting into slumber in my husband's embrace, I saw sunrays pushing through clouds to touch the earth's surface. I yawned, sighed, and decided maybe my friend wasn't out of her mind after all.

Reflection Notes

Think of a time when you have been surrounded by tragedy or crises in your life or witnessed those in the lives of others? Have you ever found yourself so sad or hurt that you are unable to see a way out? What restored you to peace? To joy? Perhaps you were uplifted by the words of a friend, a Scripture, a prayer, the touch of a loved one. Reflect and record that. And the next time you are in the dark shadows of life, hold onto what you have learned about pain and restoration.

CHAPTER 18

Keys to Freedom

"Most of us go to our grave with our music still inside us."
—Oliver Wendell Holmes

❧

FOR LORI MARCELLO

IF SOMEONE TOLD ME two years ago I would be sitting here proudly admiring my new adult second-level piano lesson book, I would have laughed out loud. But today, after a year and a half of lessons, that's exactly what I'm doing. I enjoy learning new songs, love my teacher, Miss Lori, and adore my husband for encouraging me to take the risk of realizing a dream born in my heart as a child.

Getting to this point was far from easy. The journey required reaching down deep, past childhood memories and wounds to see if I could take a chance, once more, to create music.

When I was young, I wanted to play the piano. I pestered my parents into renting one and paying for instructions. For several years I practiced most days, went to my lessons, and played in recitals. I delighted in feeling my little fingers dance upon the ivories. I dreamt of being one of those ladies I saw on TV who played in orchestras or symphonies.

In sixth grade, the music teacher asked if there were kids interested in playing in the band when we advanced to junior high school. I raised my hand and told him I played piano. All the children laughed. I looked to the teacher for explanation. He said he was referring to the marching band, and there was no room for the keyboard. His gentle response did little to soothe the sting of laughter from my classmates.

After that day, I didn't have as much enthusiasm for the piano, practiced very little, and went to lessons with less diligence than before the music teacher's comment. One afternoon, I came home and found an empty space in the living room where my piano once stood. I started crying. My mother explained money was tight and if I wasn't going to practice or go to lessons regularly, I would never improve in my playing. That meant the piano had to go.

All I heard was that I wasn't going to improve and there was no place for me and my piano in the band or at home.

Almost thirty years later I married my current husband and moved into his house where there was a piano. Every time I looked at the stringed beauty, the memories of fellow students' laughter and my lost dream returned. I asked my husband if we could get rid of the instrument. He agreed, and we began searching for a new home for the piano.

I tried online sales sites, talked to people from music stores, and even contacted a local college about donating it. Nothing worked. The piano remained in the living room, collecting dust and reminding me of a childhood failure.

In desperation, I approached a woman in my exercise class who teaches piano and asked if she knew anyone who would take this instrument for little or no money. After trying for a few weeks, she came back and said she couldn't find anyone interested. She asked if I ever played. I told her I had for a little while as a child. Then she wanted to know if I had considered playing again.

"No, no I don't think so." I hadn't allowed that thought to take residence in my consciousness.

She wanted to know why.

"I wasn't very good." There it was. I said it out loud.

"That doesn't matter. If you enjoy it, then it isn't about being good. I'd be happy to bring you on as a student if you'd like," Miss Lori told me.

I went home, sat at the piano, and began plunking out a few notes. I pulled some music books from the bench and endeavored to play a simple song. Smiling and touching the black-and-white keys with tenderness, I briefly entertained the idea of playing again. Then I shook my head and put the thought aside. It was not possible. I was too old and even if the desire to play was still in my heart, it was something I was afraid of failing at again.

When I shared my feelings with my husband, he encouraged me to think about Miss Lori's offer. Then he said, "You'll never know if you can play unless you try. God doesn't give us desires, even as children, then slam the door on our dreams. There's no failure in doing something imperfectly. The real failure is in passing up the opportunity to try doing it at all."

I hadn't considered taking this dilemma to God any more than I, for any length of time, entertained the idea of returning to the piano. But that afternoon, I sat in my prayer room, opened my heart to Him, and handed the wound of a broken dream over. It's my usual practice in my time with God to have soft music playing. I like to imagine the two of us entering into a dance while we talk. The tunes I chose were favorite Irish instrumental ballads. I relaxed, closed my eyes and waited for God to tell me how to sell the piano.

As I heard the familiar songs, He brought a memory to my mind of when I taught an adult dance class. Sometimes students shared with me that they dreamed of being dancers when they were younger. Some told me they were discouraged by others, didn't have money, or felt they just weren't good enough—so they gave up.

God reminded me how I pointed to my chest and said, "Art lives here in the heart. If your heart dreams of an avenue of expression, you have the choice to realize or deny that dream. Why not give yourself a chance to enjoy, learn, and have some fun?"

The next week I enrolled in lessons. At first I was tentative and stiff. I apologized for every mistake.

Miss Lori convinced me to lighten up. "Stop apologizing. You're just learning. You need to give yourself permission to make mistakes and have some fun with this. If it isn't going to be fun, Laura, you won't stick with it."

I soon started treating myself with gentleness. I developed tolerance for my mistakes, which I came to view as stepping stones. Progress was slow, but I kept going. Soon, I was enjoying improvement as weeks and months passed.

With time and persistence, I found a freedom in my return to piano playing. That freedom gave me permission to try other new adventures. I've dismissed the belief that I failed as a child. Taking the chance to do something I have always wanted to do changed my outlook on many things. It has shaped a new reality that includes embracing my own definition of personal success. Each new song is opportunity for growth and change as I allow my eighty-eight-keyed friend to take its rightful place in my heart and my world.

Now when I sit down to play the piano, I first thank God for not giving up on me. I praise Him for the wisdom of my husband and the tenderness of Miss Lori. Then I rejoice that

He has brought me into a new season where I'm realizing one of the life-long desires of my heart.

Reflection Notes

Do you regret letting a dream go for any reason? Do you see that dream as out of reach now because of age or what you think may be inability to accomplish it? Ask God today if He has a plan for that passion and to show you His plan to give you the desires of your heart. Then relax, learn, and enjoy.

CHAPTER 19

Commitment
or Compliance

*You know you have found your true love "When
you look into their eyes and see the person you
want to be."*
—Laura L. Padgett, *Dolores, Like the River*

FOR MARRIED COUPLES FACING FAMILY CRISES

THE MAIN REASON PEOPLE no longer want
to marry is unwillingness to commit. I heard
a TV game show host say this one day as I sat
eating popcorn and resenting myself, and my
spouse, for our inability to transform the tidal

wave of a family crisis into a glass-smooth sea of serenity. I snorted at the well-dressed, smiling celebrity as he delivered this piece of news from my little television set. What did he know?

I believed there was no couple more committed to their marriage than Keith and I. But spinning through a two-year family crisis with fear, exhaustion, and frustration had taken its toll. The truth was Keith and I were drifting apart. I felt we were going our separate ways and leaving each other behind. What good was our "commitment" doing us?

I went into my prayer room, put on soft music, and attempted to meditate and talk to God. "Why have Keith and I become strangers? What have we done wrong? We sit every morning reading Your Word and seeking ways to solve these problems. We've complied with what is expected, haven't we?"

I bowed my head and began weeping from the loneliness I felt and the burden of perceived failure. Between emotional pleas, I stared at a book I had used for research in graduate school. God brought the words of a wise adviser to mind.

"There is a difference between compliance and commitment. Anyone can show up and go through the motions. But if you want to see rewards, you need to bring more than your brain and body into life's laboratory. You must bring a committed heart."

I snapped my head up and stared straight ahead. I felt God had written the answer on the blank wall staring back at me. Keith and I were only physically showing up at prayer time. We read His Word in rote, monotone recitations, because we were completing a task that had become little more than habit. It was with our permission that problems and resentments took center stage in our morning dance with Jesus. We had tip-toed around our true feelings when talking to each other; this led to resentment.

Most important, we had lost the desire to be before the Lord, as a couple, authentically and despite troubled hearts in a terrifying journey.

The next morning as we prayed, I took Keith's hands in mine and thanked God for the husband He gave me. I asked for the Lord's guidance in taking care of our marriage and each other, as we had promised on our wedding day. I confessed my hurt, fear, and frustration to God. Then, I placed all our loved ones' lives in God's hands as I relinquished the control I mistakenly thought I had over resolutions.

This prayer pattern has become our new normal—in trials or in joys. We still come to God out of obedience to study His Word and pray. But we are now motivated by a deep yearning to spend time with Him, as a couple. We love expressing our gratitude for all His gifts, especially our union. We don't skimp on praise, and we don't hide our tears. With priorities reordered, we continue growing in a commitment to strengthen our connection to our Creator and to our marriage on this journey we choose to take together.

Reflection Notes

Are there areas of your life or the lives of loved ones where you believe you can control the outcome if you just try this or that? Can you see the toll it is taking on you, your marriage, or your family? In what ways might you find courage to relinquish the care of your loved ones into the hands of God? Ask God today to show you how to care for yourself and submit your problems or concerns to His divine intervention.

CHAPTER 20

Not My Day

You, my brothers and sisters, were called to be free. But do not use your freedom to indulge the flesh; rather, serve one another humbly in love.
—Galatians 5:13

❧

FOR GRIEVING PARENTS

BEING A GOOD STEWARD of time takes discipline to stick to schedules and not to load too many activities into one twenty-four-hour period. To ensure balance in my days, I often make a to-do list in my calendar. Although I do fairly well most days, there are times when I get lost in the hectic pace of life. It is at those times I can become resentful of any interruption or unplanned stop along the day's well-organized path. It is also at those times God has called me back to understanding what the purpose is for my days in the first place.

One morning, while waiting for my coffee pot to signal the fuel for my daily journey was ready, I took a gander out my front window. The large maple tree in my front yard has a decorative brick border around it. A woman was sitting under that tree with her back to me. I recognized her as a neighbor. Her shoulders were slumped forward, and her head was bowed.

I looked at her for a moment and considered whether or not I should go out and greet her. I hesitated because my schedule was packed, and I didn't know if I could spare the time to be neighborly. Besides, I reasoned that she might be in prayer and did not want to be interrupted.

"Oh, Lord," I groaned. "The last thing I need is to be sidetracked today. Maybe it just isn't my day."

The response was swift and clear, "Would you like to compare your agenda and demands to mine, little one?" I had no trouble understanding Whose voice that was.

I went outside, trying to figure out how I was going to work one more thing into my day, and she looked up at me. Her face was red and swollen. I asked her if she would like a drink of water. She just nodded, thanked me, and then dropped her head again. I secretly hoped this encounter wouldn't take too long.

I brought the glass of water and sat down next to her in silence for a few minutes. The brick border was wet because the sprinkler had been on earlier that morning. Ignoring my wet britches, I asked if she was okay.

"It has been a bad summer," she told me. I knew from her despondent tone and demeanor that I needed to clear my calendar.

She went on to explain that she had lost several family members in recent months, including her only son. She was in deep grief. Her tears fell as she shared the details. My tears began to fall too as the broken heart of one mother joined hands with the heart of another mother.

I've stood with several mothers as they buried their children. Through those times I have learned one very important lesson: I cannot do anything to make their circumstances better, but there are things I can do or say that will make them worse. So I resisted temptation to offer advice or smooth clichés. I just sat in the pain with her, listened, and held her hand as she unpacked layers of grief.

During our time together, among the many clouds in the sky, one cloud stayed directly overhead, releasing tiny raindrops that fell through the leaves of the giant tree and onto us. I felt the presence of God and that He too was crying for the pain of His children.

Death is part of life. As humans, we don't know when it will come or, in some cases, why. God knows the why and when for the entrance and exit of each human being. But His knowledge doesn't stop Him from hurting when we hurt.

I don't know how long we talked under that tree in the intermittent rain. I do know that her decision to stop and rest under my tree was not an interruption of my itinerary for the day. It *was* my itinerary for the day. God gave me the opportunity to return to the most important thing in this life: caring about and for others.

She finished drinking her water and said she had to go. We hugged, and she started walking up the street with her shoulders still slumped and tears still falling. When I came into the house, I picked up my devotional and began to pray. The words filled my heart as each sentence spoke to me about trusting God and giving everything to Him by offering myself in service to others.

During my prayer time, I heard Him say, "Write this experience down and share it with others."

So I did. I took the time needed to chronicle what had happened and what I learned. When I finished, it was late in the afternoon and I more fully understood that no day is "my day." It is given to me by God to do His work, on His time, for His kingdom.

I went to bed that night feeling like I had in fact done His work. And the funny thing was, I never again found my version of that day's to-do list.

Reflection Notes

As you make your plans for the day ahead, have you given God the control of how those plans will fall into place? Have you left room in your day to be available when He says, "Someone needs you today"? Have you said "thank you" when someone else has made time in their day to care for you?

CHAPTER 21

Checking My Entitlement at the Door

"An expectation is a resentment under construction."

—Anne Lamott

FOR VISION

THE CORNERS OF MY mouth drooped so low, they threatened to hook onto my collar bones. How could this be? It was mid-afternoon on Memorial Day, and my husband and I had worked hard on our latest remodeling project. We were urged to the finish line by a promise of a frozen custard blast thingy we saw advertised on TV at lunchtime. The last hour of our labor was spent in laughter and bliss as we discussed our flavorful reward. But when we went to our favorite drive-in treat shop, a voice in the speaker informed us that because of customer volume and the late afternoon hour, their custard machine stopped working. Not possible. Not fair. Custard machines don't stop working on hot summer holidays. This was an outrage.

The voice in the speaker apologized and offered a soft drink instead. I shook my head. My husband, Keith, declined the offer. As we departed I felt completely justified in my posture of pouting.

Sometimes when I'm hungry, uncomfortable and/or disappointed, I can become childlike in my outlook. What little wisdom I have accumulated over the past sixty plus years can just evaporate. It is then that the Wise One invades my heart and mind with words from other people He has sent. In this case, the verbal gems were from a woman named Vision. And believe me, this woman's name is more than appropriate considering the valuable insights she's shared with me and many others.

In conversation with her earlier in the month, Vision spoke about a person who really gets under her skin. She admitted that in the past she's had no problem letting him know exactly what he does to rile her. But on a recent encounter with him, she chose a new approach she had read or heard somewhere. My astute friend told me she asked God to bless him and change her. I thought about her words for a moment; and then confessed that for the most part I would have asked God to change him and bless me. Still there was something in Vision's prudent course of action that appealed to me.

"My new approach," Vision had said, "allowed my heart and mind to focus on God, and I was able to call on Him to help change my thinking regarding control over anyone but me."

On the drive home from the mutinous custard machine, minus at least 800 unneeded calories, I recalled Vision's words of wisdom and decided to give her technique a try. "God, bless that young lady whose face I did not see but whose voice reflected exhaustion from a busy, hot holiday shift at work. And change me—whatever that means."

Nothing happened on the spot. I was still hungry, hot, and beyond disappointed at this turn of events. After all I had expected the universe to comply with a reward I felt entitled to receive. I decided to repeat my petition a few times.

On the fourth repetition, my anger lessened, and I actually had compassion for the woman delivering this devastating news. I found it hard to be upset with someone while calling blessings upon them.

The "change me part" took a little longer. When my displeasure subsided and my focus shifted, I asked myself exactly how important the frozen custard blast thingy was anyway. Was this something I should allow to break the spirit of an otherwise good, productive, and peaceful day? I also questioned my expectation that things should work out according to my plans.

The words of my friend proved to be more than a mantra eliminating discomfort. Vision's strategy showed me I have control over my attitudes and outlooks even if I'm in a funk. But control over other people, events, and even machines? No. That is not available.

I realized my friend's new philosophy of "bless them and change me," was my ticket back to good humor, peace, and serenity. I now rate this at the top of my list of spiritual options. That feels a whole lot better than any sweet treat on life's menu.

With clearer thinking and less pouting, I saw the real problem at hand: hunger. With what was left of our energy, Keith and I got busy and put together Ma Padgett's killer tacos. Just as peace and serenity provide healthy ways for my mind and soul to function, I suspect the tacos were the better choice to feed my little physical self.

Sometimes God uses circumstances, words from friends, or just plain good sense to return me to healthy living. But this requires listening, being grateful for the wise words of others, and letting go of "my way" thinking. It also is a good idea to go to the frozen custard place *before* they run out of treats.

Reflection Notes

Can you think of a time when you were disappointed
and flew off the handle, or just became angry on
the inside and spent time resenting someone or a
situation? Did you ever go to God for an attitude
adjustment? He is the great spiritual chiropractor.
Perhaps He offered a new outlook through the wise
words of a trusted friend. How did the adjustment
make the situation feel or look different?

CHAPTER 22

At the Foot of the Cross

Be strong and courageous. Do not be afraid or terrified because of them, for the LORD your God goes with you; he will never leave you nor forsake you.

—Deuteronomy 31:6

FOR CONNIE KOPROWICZ, BEVERLEY EWERS, MOLLY WEGENER, JUDY JOYCE, REBECCA ZIMMERMAN

IN THE FAITH-BASED WORLD, there are few experiences as rewarding as offering ourselves fully to God by moving into a centered awareness of His presence. Some people call this prayer. Others identify it as praise. Still others define this as worship.

Dance is one special and meaningful way for me to participate in all the above. Many years in dance training have given me expertise to lead workshops, dance in church services, and present at gatherings, festivals, and conferences. The formal name for dancing in church is "liturgical dance." I prefer to call it "sacred dance" because we interpret more than liturgy; and more than once I've been told a movement piece touched a sacred space in another's heart.

The revival of sacred dance in modern-day church service is controversial. In the past I have been shy about putting it forward as a form of worship art. Not everyone sees dance as appropriate for church and on occasion, when asked to share the dance in church, I've declined because I feared offending others.

Then at the beginning of one Lenten season, I learned to answer God's call no matter what my shyness, fears, or critics dictate. God showed me that He gives each person gifts to use for the benefit of others, and He has a plan for just how that works, separate from worldly approval.

Three weeks before Lent began, the worship leader in my church asked the dance team to offer a specific dance at the Ash Wednesday evening service. I listened to the song he selected and heard each verse speaking into brokenness and laying guilt and burdens at the foot of the cross. I felt there couldn't have been a more meaningful expression of repentance and acceptance of God's love.

The week before Ash Wednesday was riddled with obstacles. It was hard to get rehearsals together. The costumes the team agreed upon were difficult to find. Additionally, one of my knees was swollen and painful. In exasperation one evening, I told the worship leader it simply wasn't coming together, and we would have to scrap the dance. He reluctantly agreed to remove it from the order of service.

I was unable to sleep the night before Ash Wednesday. After an hour or so, I got up, read and prayed. I asked God why I was awake. His message was clear. The dance was to be done. Someone would be there in need of His message through movement. The next morning I made the necessary calls to get the dance piece put back in the worship service. With the help of a talented costume maker and the enthusiasm of the gifted dance team, God provided all we needed to honor the call He had sent.

At the appointed time in the service, the dancers offered praise, prayer, and worship through the gift God had given and asked us to share. The piece typically brings many people (including the dancers) to tears, as they experience this story in movement.

I felt energy surge through my body and out to the audience as I moved. I departed from my choreographed solo portion, allowing my body to sway and turn in response to leading from an invisible dance partner. Miraculously my body felt limber as my arms rose while my knees bent before the cross. I flowed through pain-free movements demonstrating release and relief.

After dancing, I returned to my seat and kept my heart focused on worship. I prayed, "Lord, I trust You and ask Your forgiveness for my reluctance to obey. Whatever You're going to do tonight, I thank You."

The sacrament of Holy Communion followed the dance. A teenage girl and another woman went forward to the altar. The young lady knelt, placed her face in her hands, and began to weep. Her companion held her as they accepted the bread and wine. My heartbeat quickened. I sat forward in the chair with my eyes fastened on the couple. I didn't know them. I didn't know their trouble. Yet, I swayed under the burden of their palpable anguish.

Leaving the sanctuary in silence and with my vision directed downward, I almost missed seeing the same young woman sitting in a back-row seat. Before exiting the room, I looked behind me and over my shoulder. When our eyes connected, she mouthed the words, "Thank you."

Still sobbing, she slumped into the arms of her companion. The other woman drew her close and kissed her forehead.

I've never seen either woman again. I still have no information about their suffering. Yet, I know with certainty that when God gifts us, He does not do it for our own use. He expects us to use our gifts for the good, support, and maybe even healing of others. He answers our obedience with blessings of support and healing for us too.

While on this earth, I will never know for sure if that young woman was the one God intended to reach in the service that night. That was God's work. My work was to obey and share His message of hope and healing. And I guess you could say on that particular Ash Wednesday, out of obedience that unseated misgivings, I placed my own hesitation and fear at the foot of the cross.

Reflection Notes

When has God called you to carry His work to another and you felt inadequate or fearful? Take a few minutes and ask Him to help you recall that time and how He walked you into surrendering to His will, despite human objections. It may help you move forward today if you are facing a task that seems beyond your own confidence or ability.

CHAPTER 23

Thy Kingdom Come

"Most Christians glibly recite 'Thy kingdom come,' but this means almost nothing until and unless they also say, 'my kingdom go'."
—Father Richard Rohr

❧

FOR THE VICTIMS OF THE AURORA THEATER
AND COLUMBINE HIGH SCHOOL SHOOTINGS

"THERE'S BEEN A SHOOTING at an Aurora, Colorado theater, leaving several dead and dozens wounded." The voice from NPR woke me at 6:30 a.m. I jolted out of a deep sleep I'd been enjoying for only a few hours.

Had I heard correctly? Another violent tragedy invaded my home state. Memories of the 1999 Columbine massacre surfaced, uninvited.

I stumbled to my kitchen and turned on the television. No, I was not suffering auditory hallucinations in a sleep-deprived stupor. Local news anchors confirmed the report. In the next two days, victims were named. Those killed ranged from six to fifty-one years old. More victims remained in hospitals. Heaviness of hearts grew, and grief multiplied on individual, communal, national, and global levels.

"How will we cope, Lord? What can we do?" I choked out my morning prayers as tears flowed without ceasing. "God, is this our world now? How will any of us be able to cope, Lord?"

In worship service on the Sunday following the shootings, our pastor described a prayer vigil she attended for the victims. She was part of a group gathered in shock and confusion, looking for answers, praying for hope. The vigil was held on a hilltop overlooking the theater. Her words painted an image of that collection of strangers brought together by tragedy but held together by faith, as they prayed the Lord's Prayer in one voice. As she recounted the prayer she placed particular emphasis on the words "Thy kingdom come."

The rest of that week, I couldn't shake the phrase, "Thy kingdom come." As a Christian, I repeat this prayer often but, admittedly, am not always considering all the implications of what that means. Never before had I felt the impact of that phrase with such intensity. I asked God to show me what His kingdom really might look like on earth. This is the vision He gave me:

"My kingdom comes with my Son's inclusive light shining on all without discriminating by color, doctrine, nationality, gender, status, ability, or politics.

"My kingdom comes by following my Son's instruction to take personal responsibility for co-creating a world of love, respect, and care for all life forms.

"My kingdom comes with intentional celebration of diversity and similarity with joy.

"My kingdom comes with the offering of smiles to the stranger and outstretched hands to the outsider.

"My kingdom comes by knowing the cost of loving, but still choosing to love because that is all that matters.

"My kingdom comes bathed in my Son's peace that will pass all human understanding."

That evening I reflected on the pastor's words again. The final words in her sermon were, "Thy Kingdom comes most times outside of a pretty liturgical space, and in this, yes even in this, the middle of a crime scene."

Then I offered a pain-laden prayer to the Colorado summer sky. "Oh yes, Lord, please. Let Thy kingdom come today, to me, to us, and to all. This is how we will cope."

Reflection Notes

In a world full of misunderstanding, intolerance, and violence, how do you see yourself modeling God's kingdom of acceptance, tolerance, and love? What does His kingdom look like from your lens? Can you see places where you can begin to contribute to a more unified and uplifting community?

CHAPTER 24

We Came to Play

This is the day the LORD has made; we will rejoice and be glad in it.
—Psalm 118:24, NKJV

❧

FOR MAYOR MARJORIE SLOAN, GOLDEN, COLORADO

THE FLATBED TRUCK, ADORNED with shiny tinsel and silver bells, crawled along Golden, Colorado's Main Street as part of an annual parade announcing the Christmas Season's arrival. It stopped along the route to allow gathered spectators photo opportunities. This early December event is a ritual I've been part of for over five years. My role may seem odd to some but, you see, my friends and I are elves.

The elves have been at the center of these crowds on many occasions. For the most part, I feel comfortable performing as an elf in front of thousands of strangers. That year was different. Our country had experienced an escalation of violent attacks, mostly perpetrated in crowds. Stories filled news feeds, one after another, of shooters delivering death and destruction from San Bernardino to Colorado Springs.

To say I was a little nervous on that exposed flatbed elf-wagon would be like Noah coming off the Ark and calling his experience the result of a minor cloudburst. I didn't want to alarm my elf mates, so I kept smiling and waving as I diligently watched the crowd for possible threats. More than once I breathed a sigh of relief upon spying a uniformed law enforcement officer in the crowd.

In all my years as an elf, I couldn't remember feeling so uncomfortable, and vulnerable, as we helped our community usher in a season typically associated with cheer and good will. I wondered why I had gathered my friends and neighbors, dressed them in crazy outfits, and marched them into what could be considered harm's way. I was mentally bringing my pointy-shod feet up to my velvet-clad backside and delivering a swift kick to myself for being so careless with the safety of others.

I recalled a conversation I had with a friend about the dangerous times in which we live. He told me he found it hard to go anywhere in public without feeling exposed to attack and had become wary of strangers or unfamiliar surroundings. Then a familiar voice in my right ear, barely audible above the crowd noise, pulled me out of my gloomy musings. The voice belonged to a lady I've been honored to share the spotlight with in many previous Golden Christmas Parades. My face registered surprise—not at her voice but her words. It was as if she read my thoughts.

"This is exactly what we need today!" She smiled and nodded at me.

Without missing a beat, she continued waving her holiday greetings to the spectators. I'm pretty sure no one else on the truck heard her speak. Three elves belted out a Christmas carol in their best imitation of a Super Bowl half-time show. The crowd erupted in appreciative cheers, laughter, and applause. I recognized the wisdom of her words and knew she was right.

Thousands of people refused to be confined or restricted by the threat of terrorism. Children and adults gathered to be part of a small-town tradition despite the potential harm others may choose to inflict. As I gazed on the people gathered, I released my need to comb the onlookers for uniforms. Instead I soaked up the shared joy on the upturned, rosy-cheeked faces of my neighbors, young and old. I rested in appreciation of a little town reflecting loud and joyous rebellion against being held hostage in chains of fear.

I felt my elf heart burst with gratitude for being invited to share in their party. I was proud to live in a community that chose to collectively resist the oppression of "what if's" that could have kept us hiding in our basements while handing over our freedom to others.

I turned to the lady on my right and said, "Yes, ma'am, Mayor. This is exactly what we needed. And today, we came to play."

Reflection Notes

Have you ever felt fear choking joy out of an activity or event? If so, how did you handle the situation? Were you able to feel God's comfort or hear His words through Scripture or perhaps the words of another person?

CHAPTER 25

Fish Tale

Then Peter got down out of the boat, walked on the water and came toward Jesus. But when he saw the wind, he was afraid and, beginning to sink, cried out, "Lord, save me!"
—Matthew 14:29-30

❧

FOR CARLA PARKS

AFTER TWO HOURS OF snagging my line, breaking hooks, slipping on rocks, hauling in weeds and sticks covered with matter I knew was breathing, I was more than a little discouraged. This particular fishing trip had proven to be beyond disappointing. It was hard to keep resentment at bay when I remembered I was missing my Saturday ballet class.

My husband instructed me for months on the finer points of catching fish. But we were having no luck on the Eagle River in western Colorado that day. He decided we should separate and he headed downstream to try his luck in a new spot. I was planning to quit fishing for the day after one last cast of my anemic bait.

I hurled the line into the water and felt it strike something. Thinking the hook once again jammed in the rocks, I tugged in an attempt to dislodge it. The line moved away from me.

It appeared I had a fish. I did what Keith taught me and pulled back hard, setting the hook. The fish jumped out of the water, demonstrating he did not qualify as a small-fry. He was a strong fighter and pulled me into deep, fast-moving water. My body tensed as I attempted to find flat rocks that could provide solid footing.

I frantically waved in Keith's direction. He returned the wave, gave a slow nod, and continued moving away. I gave more hand motions. He kept moving until he was out of sight around a river bend.

"No, no, no. I'm in real trouble here!" I yelled, but the roaring water muted my words. I was on my own with a killer fish, fast current, and deepening cold water. I wished I were in Miss Carla's dance class.

Panic rose and I searched for anything that could give me a fighting chance. I reminded Jesus that although He could walk on water, that talent was not anywhere in my personal repertoire.

"Help, Lord. Save me. I have no idea what to do here. Please send a sign, a signal, or even a vision of how to get out of this mess."

I figured roaring water or not, God could hear the desperate pleas of one of His kids.

My ballet training seeped into my mind and muscles along with the image of my teacher, Miss Carla, drumming instructions into her students week after week. I tried to focus on those images instead of the frigid thigh-high water.

"Keep your feet shoulder-width apart and flat. Toes out. Knees slightly bent. Tuck your backside under and pull your gut in. Shoulders back and down; they don't make good earrings. Chin up, strong and proud. Tighten, tighten and hold. Keeping your feet firmly planted and your body aligned in a balanced posture will serve you well in all walks of life, not just dance.

"Now breathe, breathe, and breathe. How do you expect to stay alive if you don't breathe?" Miss Carla's words seemed to be winning the battle over the deafening voice of the river. Staying alive, however, was not a certainty in my view. I looked to the sky to thank God for the supernatural words of Carla.

Dancers don't take time to analyze technical details once learned. We depend on muscle memory as a sort of physical teleprompter. With Miss Carla directing and my muscles obeying, I began to feel the familiar tension and strength needed to remain upright.

Intermingled with Miss Carla's words were Keith's directions from prior fishing expeditions. "Let the line out a little when you feel it go taut. Give the fish room to run. That'll tire him out. Keep the pole pointed upward to hold tension on the line. Reel him in slowly, but let him have his fight."

Keeping my stance as Miss Carla commanded, I also worked at practicing proper fishing technique and keeping myself in the fight, or rather dance. Maybe it was my fierce competitive nature or plain old-fashioned stubbornness that kept the idea of just dropping the pole altogether from entering my mind.

Without warning, the line went limp. I wondered if my dance partner left the stage. I relaxed my stance, according to Miss Carla's advice to rest when possible. I came to a fully upright position and took a deep breath. The fish took advantage of my less tense posture. He was off and running (swimming actually) again. I wasted no time moving back into proper ballet form with Miss Carla's directives acting as melody and Keith's words providing rhythm for the performance.

"I can tell when you're not sucking in that gut, Padgett. Pull it in. Tuck that bum under and find your center. You can keep your balance by bending your knees slightly and making sure your feet are shoulder-width apart. Breathe, breathe, breathe girl." I welcomed the repetitive nature of elemental instruction. It was as if Miss Carla was in the water with me.

It felt like I struggled for hours, although I've no idea how long the bout actually lasted. Prior to my complete physical collapse, my husband appeared with a net and lifted the great river monster from the water. I'll never know how he knew to come to my aid. Maybe a life-saving angel tapped him on the shoulder and called attention to my distress. Perhaps the pointing (and probably laughing) aimed in my direction from the fishermen on the opposite river bank alerted him to my predicament.

Keith emitted a low whistle and declared, "Wow, what a beauty!" Since I was standing with my hat askew, up to my knees in river muck, and sweating like an exhausted marathon runner, I was pretty sure he wasn't referring to his bride.

"Good job, Laura. What do you want to do? He has to weigh at least three pounds."

I fell flat on my rump on the sandy bank at the river's edge. With screaming muscles and eyes surveying what could have been a watery coffin, I asked for clarification. "Do? What do I want to do? Being close to land, breathing almost normally, and realizing I may yet see another day seems to be working just fine for now."

"No, Honey. I mean do you want to keep him or throw him back?" He was looking at our finned friend resting in shallow water at the river's edge.

"I hadn't thought that far ahead to tell the truth." I let go of the fishing pole that had been an extension of my right arm until my spouse rescued me. I leaned back on my elbows for support on the shore while my husband and three other fishing folks admired the fruits of my labor. All I wanted was a hot bath and my bed.

Experience has taught me God will bring help when we need it, even if He works through worldly directives that He drops into our minds at the right time. I knew my husband's expertise helped me land that fish. I told him that as we drove home, after placing our mini sea beast on ice to await his honored place at our dinner table.

However, I will never doubt Miss Carla's persistent classroom instructions made a significant contribution to my ability to live, and fish, another day. As promised, her directives proved to be valuable outside of her dance studio.

Before retiring that night, I thanked God for his faithful care in what could have been an embarrassing and even dangerous situation. Then I set about writing the most heartfelt thank you note I've ever penned. It began, "Dear Miss Carla."

Reflection Notes

I usually rely on my devotionals, Bible studies and words from Christian friends to provide direction. But sometimes God has used lessons learned in a secular setting to bring about a miraculous outcome. How about you? Can you think of a time you were prompted to recall something or maybe someone who contributed to a successful ending in a tough situation?

About the Author

LAURA PADGETT is an award-winning author, dancer, and sought after public speaker. Her short piece "Mama's Ring" won second place in a nationwide writing contest held by Xulon Press, and her story "One Foot and Then the Other" won honorable mention out of over five thousand submissions in the 2017 Writer's Digest Short Story Competition. Two of the pieces in this anthology, "It's for Everyone" and "Silver and Gold" have appeared in *Chicken Soup for the Soul* publications. "Mama's Ring" along with "Thy Kingdom Come" were published in Xulon Press's *Letters to America*.

Her first book, *Dolores, Like the River*, published in 2013 by Westbow Press, chronicles her thirty-five-year relationship with her mentor, Dolores. In it, she shares her journey to find Jesus and her entrance into recovery from the effects of child abuse and alcoholic parents.

Padgett has been a speaker and presenter at women's retreats, workshops, and dance festivals for over fifteen years. Her presentations and workshops focus on teaching others how to tell their stories in writing and how to dance in praise, prayer, and worship to the Lord Jesus Christ.

Padgett lives in Lakewood, Colorado with Keith, her husband of twenty-five years. She has one son (Gabriel), two stepchildren (Laurie and Orin), and three grandchildren (Tom, Katie, and Sophia).

If you enjoy these stories, please visit Laura's website at lauralpadgett.com and click on the link to her blog, "Livin' What You're Given," where she offers stories of encouragement, transformation, and inspiration through the lenses of experience, faith, and humor. You can also find her on her Facebook author page at: https://www.facebook.com/ LauraLPadgettAuthorSpeakerDancer.

Dolores, Like the River

In a time when the world appears to worship all things youthful, sometimes aging is seen as synonymous with diminished value and purpose. Dolores was sixty-five years old, had raised two children, taught hundreds, and was enjoying peaceful retirement years, with her life's partner, in a sleepy mountain town in western Colorado. Then she met Laura, who was in her mid-twenties. God had a purpose for bringing these two women together. As you follow the narrative of their thirty-five-year relationship, it may change the way you see beauty and purpose in aging.

Available at Amazon.com

Westbow Press.com, and BN.com

ISBN: 9781490814384

CHAPTER 1

On the Run

"ARE YOU OUT OF your mind?" Lana, one of my friends and coworkers, sat in disbelief. I had announced my intention to move from the sprawling metropolis of Denver. My plan was to relocate to Montrose, a small town in the middle of a valley and farmland on the western side of the Continental Divide in Colorado.

She fired question after question. "What can possibly interest you in some little mountain town? What life can that place offer someone in her twenties with a good job? How can it compare with living in a city with limitless artistic, educational, and cultural benefits?"

"Look, I have already explained this," I replied patiently. "I need to get away from here, and I need a change, period. I have a job waiting for me there."

Frankly, I was getting weary of well-meaning people demanding explanations from me. I was over twenty-five years old. I didn't owe anyone anything. I made it this far without anyone's help, and I was fully competent to continue on with my life. The interference and unsolicited advice was becoming intolerable.

"How will you move? How will you take your stuff over there?" She wanted to know some of the details. I found that encouraging.

"Well, that's where I am hoping for some help from my friends," I admitted. I was grateful Lana was moving away from inquiring about my motives and my sanity. The new conversational direction gave me opportunity to ask for her assistance. I was counting on the fact that Lana rarely resisted opportunities to participate in novel exploits.

I lit a cigarette and continued unfolding my plans. "I'm selling some belongings. The place I'm renting is fully furnished. My old Chevy will carry some of my worldly goods. Since you have a large van, I am asking you to transport the other things I plan to keep. I'll pay for gas and food."

"Okay," she said, "but why Montrose? What is over there that interests you? Laura, I'm going to miss you. It does sound like a fun adventure, but are you sure? I mean you just started back to school and are dating a really cool guy. What about all that?"

"I don't think that relationship is what I really want; and as I keep saying, I need to get away from here and away from my mother. I've put up with her last hurtful stunt. I don't care if she is a drunk. That is her choice, and drinking has always been more important to her than her family. I just need to find my own life without worrying about bailing her out of jail or plucking her off the streets. I'm tired of the vomit, the drunken friends, and the midnight calls to rescue her. I've seen all the dumps on Larimer Street that I care to in this lifetime, thank you." I stubbed out one cigarette and lit another.

After a few minutes of silence, I stopped trying to persuade her. "Look, if helping me is a problem for you, forget it. I'll get there with what I can carry in my car," I said. I tried to make my voice reflect the resolve in my heart and gut. No one was going to stop this move.

"All right, I'll help you. But you still haven't answered my question. How did you decide on Montrose?" she asked.

I told her I answered an advertisement in a trade magazine for employment. When I went to the job interview, the little town looked like a perfect place for what I hoped would be a new start. It was small, quaint, in the middle of beautiful country, and 250 miles from my current home and my mother. Lana shrugged and again assured me she would assist with my move.

I was relieved. Moving was one thing, but leaving all of my worldly belongings behind was something altogether different. For a moment, as I talked this through with her, I felt sadness for leaving my life in Denver, especially because my two sisters lived there. I couldn't think about that now. I had to go. I had to.

On the Saturday of my departure, several people, including my sisters, were there to help with the final loading. No one seemed to share my enthusiasm for my newly chosen direction. I put their feelings and objections aside. I was leaving, period. They could come and visit any time they wanted, or not.

The trip from Denver to Montrose took about five hours. I drove a 1950 Chevy sedan I had won in a bet when the Pittsburgh Steelers beat the Dallas Cowboys in the 1976 Super Bowl. My jalopy was loaded with records, stuffed toys, clothes, a few plants, and several cartons of Marlboros. The rest of my worldly goods preceded me out of town, in the van.

I was born and raised in Denver, but my family spent little to no time playing in the nearby mountains. My father had a heart condition that made it difficult to breathe in higher altitudes. Denver's elevation, at one mile above sea level, was about all he could take in the years before his death at age fifty-six. My mother usually complained of motion sickness and didn't like traveling on the winding roads over mountain passes. For me, the mountain scenery was no more recognizable than it would have been to a first-time Colorado visitor.

There were, however, some familiar spots along the journey out of town. A memory of one picnic near the small town of Bailey, off

Highway 285, came to mind. I remembered Papa coming to get me out of a tree when I climbed too high and cried for rescue. He laughed and teased me but had no problem responding to the pleas of his middle child. There were times my dad could be very tender and gentle. But I was hard-pressed to find a lot of those warm, fuzzy memories.

I thought there were probably *some* good things about being in a family but, personally, I had developed a preference for flying solo. Refusing to be melancholy about leaving Denver behind, I focused on the September landscape.

In the fall, Colorado high country is fantastic. The aspen trees dance on the breeze as they shamelessly swirl their multicolored frocks. Little creeks appear from time to time along the winding roads and add voices to nature's concert, in support of the trees' choreography. Copious amounts of green, gold, and brown wild grasses rustle in response to grazing by small and large creatures.

We made our way over Kenosha Pass and descended onto a long stretch of road running through Park County. The area is called South Park. This particular piece of land, for the most part, is flat and supports ranches. A keen eye can pick up the graceful form of an antelope sharing feeding ground with cattle and sheep. Fields are populated with an array of fall wild flowers. All this open space rests in the shadows of the rugged Rocky Mountains. Towering, treeless peaks sport snowcaps that serve as headgear year-round.

The beauty caused my breath to catch in my throat. The doubts that incessantly played as background music in my mind were momentarily silenced. Truly, this was a good decision. This was the right decision.

Lana and I stopped to stretch our legs about halfway through the park. "This is like a completely different world. This is where you are going to live, Laura. Maybe this isn't such a stupid idea after all. It's beautiful," she announced.

"Yeah, thanks. I know. But this isn't exactly my destination. That's over a pass or two yet," I informed her.

She didn't hear me. She was busy snapping pictures in every direction. I pulled out a cigarette, lit it, blew out the match, and put the spent fire implement in my jacket pocket. My father had always said that careless humans were usually responsible for forest and wild grass fires. On the rare occasions when I found myself out of doors, my father's words served to keep me in proper ecological posture.

A different world was right. I hadn't seen so much open land in a very long time. The smell of the fields and the sight of the looming mountains provided a calming balm over my hesitant heart that waxed and waned between righteous certainties of my new direction and viewing each passing mile in the light of loss. I missed my sisters already. I felt guilty about leaving my mother without telling her what was going on or even calling to say good-bye. I took a long drag on my cigarette.

"She is not my responsibility. She chose her life. Let her live it. I am going to live mine," I said out loud to the silent and seemingly understanding mountain range bordering the park.

After we made our way through South Park, we climbed, crossed, and descended Monarch Pass. The forested areas held my attention and provided return to the positive swing of the pendulum of uncertainty. There was cleanliness about these surroundings. The aged pine trees exuded a strength that testified to their resilience and determination in the face of the severe Colorado winters. I hoped this pristine yet rugged environment would wash away my past.

Arriving in Montrose evoked squeals of delight from my traveling companion. "Wow, this place is gorgeous. Can you just imagine all the pictures you can take? And look, there's a restaurant and everything," Lana observed.

"Good," I snarled. "I need a beer. I hope this place isn't dry."

The five-hour drive from Denver to Montrose was accompanied only by soft drinks as liquid sustenance. Drinking and driving terrified me. The memories never seemed to fade of the accidents and DUIs my mother had racked up, not to mention expenses for bailing her out of jail. Then there were the court appearances. But that was all behind me now. She could bail herself out, appear before judges solo, and deal with her own accidents and the financial disasters resulting from her choices. I was free—free from her and free from my past. She couldn't hurt me now.

Lana and I ate, drank, and then found the little apartment I was renting. After unloading my car, we took off in the old Chevy to explore the town. To our delight, there were several bars and dancing establishments.

"This will do nicely," I said. "This will do nicely, indeed."

The next morning, Lana headed home, but not before I treated her to breakfast at one of the local greasy spoons. During breakfast, she said it seemed like I already knew my way around and was going to do just fine.

I let her leave without telling her that I, in fact, had been to Montrose while in high school for a sporting event. She didn't need to know that my parents were from Grand Junction, just an hour north, and that on trips to the Junction my family had driven through this little spot many times. It wasn't important to inform her that this was a frequent trip for my father and his three daughters when he needed to deposit us for a few weeks with family while he searched for our wayward mother. Although Montrose was to be my new home, returning to Grand Junction with its memories of fear and abandonment did *not* factor into my plans.

After breakfast, I watched my friend drive toward the highway leading back to Denver. I tried to silence the sad, little voice protesting that the last contact to my old life was heading back to the Mile High City without me. The seesaw of feelings, with positive affirmation on one side and guilt with trepidation on the other, was getting old. I swallowed hard and reminded myself I was finally free. That was the biggest positive imaginable in my book.

After waving to Lana's rearview mirror, I lit a cigarette, popped the top on a fresh beer, and walked into my new life.

Made in the USA
San Bernardino, CA
04 September 2018